Living inside the Revolution

An Irish woman in Cuba

Karen McCartney

Copyright © 2015 Karen McCartney
All rights reserved
ISBN–10: 1511958162
ISBN-13: 978-1511958165

PROLOGUE

What follows is a purely personal account of events and conversations that took place over the six years I spent living in Cuba, from 1999-2005. The present tense is used throughout in order to create a sense of immediacy and vitality, as a bridge between the present and the events as they were experienced at the time.

Many of the names and some of the details of individuals featuring in the narrative have been changed - when I thought it was important to protect their anonymity - while others have not.

I owe an immense debt of gratitude to all the characters whose lives cross these pages for opening up to me and for welcoming me into a society with which very few foreigners have had the opportunity to become as closely acquainted as I am.

All rights reserved
Copyright © 2015 Karen McCartney

No part of this publication can be reproduced or transmitted in any form whatsoever, or by any means, electronic or mechanical, without the express permission in writing of Karen McCartney.

Karen McCartney

CONTENTS

1. Prologue — 3
2. Introduction — 8
3. Life At Granma — 17
4. Now What Do I Do? — 32
5. The Three S's — 48
6. On The Road — 64
7. Santería And The Spirits — 78
8. Between The Frying Pan And The Fire — 92
9. Life In Jaimanitas — 108
10. Manicures In The Mountains — 134
11. What Can You Do For Me? — 159
12. Epilogue — 177
13. A Brief History Of The Revolution — 185
14. Key Dates In The Revolution — 192
15. Explanatory Notes On Some Of The Organisations Mentioned In This Book — 196

El hombre no se mide por las veces que se cae,
si no por las que se levanta
The measure of a man is not in the number of times he falls, but in the number of times he gets up (Author's translation)
José Martí

This book is dedicated to the determination of the Cuban people to survive.

Acknowledgements
My deepest thanks to Douglas Hamilton, Roisin Shannon, Alan Munton, Helen Barnes, Paul Clements, Jesús Noguera, Charlie Rosenberg and Vinko Kalcic for their help and support.

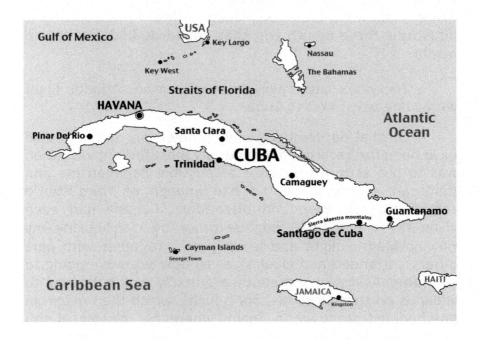

Introduction

THE BEGINNING

Never again! Those were my last words, and I said them audibly, as I stepped on board a Cubana Aviation flight at José Martí International airport. It was September 1987 and I was leaving Havana that evening, vowing that on no account would I return to Cuba, or indeed Central America, after a disastrous three-month trip that ended as badly as it had begun.

Ten years later I was to board a trans-Atlantic flight with a one-way ticket to Cuba.

On that September evening, however, nothing could have been further from my mind. My most fervent wish then was to put as much distance as possible between me and that part of the globe. I'd had enough of Third World corruption, confusion and discomfort. Cubana had even given the trip a final *coup de grace* by overbooking my Havana-Madrid flight and leaving me - together with nine others - stranded and clueless as to how we were going to get home. As it was, somebody eventually took a decision to allow us on to a Moscow-bound flight, which then made an unscheduled stopover in Spain, where our cluster of ten hastily disembarked. Strictly only the ten of us. We had to squeeze past security guards mounted on the doors of the plane to ensure that none of the Cuban or Russian passengers made an impromptu bid to savour western hospitality.

That visit to Cuba was a contingency arrangement. My plan had never been to holiday on the island. I'd gone to Central America two months earlier to express my solidarity with the Sandinista revolution in Nicaragua by joining a work brigade. My solidarity, however, evaporated within days of arriving in the country, vanquished by heat, insects, diarrhoea and the relentlessly tedious agricultural work I had volunteered for. Weeding black beans and clumping through mud in humid tobacco barns gave me plenty of opportunities to reflect on the wisdom of having travelled so far to endure so much.

Hardship and poverty were much more entrenched and widespread than I could have ever imagined. The reality I was encountering daily appalled me, and rarely fitted into my simplistic expectations of what could be achieved by a band of armed guerrilla fighters taking on the responsibilities of government with good intentions. All over the country health, education and agricultural projects were failing as a consequence of the U.S. blockade and the strength of the Contra offensive. Funds originally set aside for these initiatives were being diverted into weapons needed for defence. Half-built schools and empty medical stores spelt out the defeat of the Revolution. It was deeply depressing.

At the same time, questions were simmering about how good those initial intentions really were. Rumours of corruption among party cadres filtered through to the international brigades, casting a shadow over our view of the leadership. Locals openly called all westerners gringos, often disparagingly so, despite our protestations that we were Europeans on a good will visit. This latter piece of information was often greeted with a smirk, particularly if the local in question happened to be a Ray Ban-wearing landowner driving a 4 Wheel Drive. As the days went by, a sense of futility weighed upon me. Nothing I could do would move this revolution forward even a centimetre. To believe otherwise was self delusion.

Rather than risk my disappointment turning into cynicism, I decided to return to my comfortable life in Spain earlier than planned. That plan was thwarted. On the day I travelled into Managua to change my flight dates, all my money, my passport and my airline tickets were stolen. Like it or not, I had to remain in Nicaragua until replacements were obtained. It took one month and I bitterly resented every day of that month. I felt penned in, prisoner in a country which seemed to be bent on teaching me a lesson about the naiveté of my political beliefs ... and about the limits of my physical endurance. At night cockroaches clicked across the tiled floors of our rooms, mosquitoes droned in the darkness, and every morning I woke to find new batches of ugly red lumps, where fleas had feasted, on my thighs and stomach.

My "role" in the Sandinista revolution remained firmly back stage. I drifted about in the wings of that hot and humid hellhole of a country full of doubts and self-loathing. I felt uncomfortable with my tendency to be increasingly critical and I despised my bourgeois inability to withstand the hardships of life in Central America. For years I'd followed events in Nicaragua and dreamed of being a first-hand witness to the revolution that I had supported both ideologically and practically with whatever fundraising activities I could organise and participate in. Now I was there, I was miserable.

Seeing my mood, Cristina, my travelling companion, suggested that we "live it up" in Cuba before returning to Spain. Her suggestion did indeed cheer me, if only because it meant I wasn't returning home so disgracefully early that I would have to admit defeat.

"Yes, let's live it up. Let's spend a couple of weeks in Cuba," I said, thinking that maybe a "mature and developed revolution" would be more my style, whatever my style was. I was confused and exhausted. I just wanted a clean bed to sleep in and the certainty that my money would be where I'd left it when I woke in the morning.

The Managua- Havana flight took almost two hours. Just before the aircraft doors closed I spotted President Daniel Ortega and key members of his cabinet hurrying across the tarmac to join us. The Cuban flight attendant leaned over and whispered to us that they were travelling to

Havana to meet Fidel Castro to discuss a major peace agreement (Esquipulas II) for Central America. Once the flight was airborne, Cristina and I pleaded with her to inquire whether he would consider giving us his autograph. He agreed. During the five minutes or so we chatted to him, Ortega expressed his profound thanks to us for having spent time in Nicaragua on a solidarity mission. He looked me in the eye and spoke of his hope that I, and others like me, would return again soon because his country needed international support. Then he autographed a note which I gave him ending with the words, *"Long Live the Sandinista Revolution"*.

As I made my way down the aisle toward my seat, shame and disappointment weighed upon the initial elation I'd experienced on meeting Daniel Ortega. I was ashamed at my duplicity because I was, after all, slinking out of the country because I'd had enough. I'd discovered that the limits to my solidarity were only as far away as the next flea bite, rumour or smirk. Regrets about having wasted a unique opportunity to get close to an historic event, to get inside it, began to gnaw at me. I felt empty inside, lacking in confidence and bereft of political ideals.

Cuba was paradise after the hardships endured in Nicaragua. Clean running water, crisp cotton sheets, hotel menus, uniformed bell boys and a gentle island breeze allowed me to suspend my ruminations and confusion for the time being. The only dark cloud was that almost everywhere we went, Cristina and I were harassed by young men keen for a date, keen, no doubt, for a wife and a European passport. Hustlers targeted us in the vicinity of dollar shops, in the hope that we'd buy them an iron or even a washing machine. The siege, annoying as it was, at least distracted me from the mass of doubts and contradictions that were still clouding my mind.

My toleration of these minor "inconveniences" snapped the moment a uniformed Cubana representative politely — but firmly - disclosed that we had been overbooked and were not leaving that night. Cristina and I were standing at the check-in desk, limp tickets in hand, luggage at our feet. Our excitement turned to anger and helplessness in a matter of seconds. We protested and continued protesting even as the roar above our heads told us that "our flight" had departed. Two days of uncertainty were to pass before we were bussed back to the airport and herded onto the Moscow-bound flight.

Ten years after my return from Nicaragua, I had found work as a freelance journalist in Belfast, and was also deeply involved in community education projects in one of the more marginalised areas of the city. Both jobs were satisfying and I learned a lot, but I began to feel restless and fearful of the lure of a comfortable routine in which the months become years, and the years, decades. My fortieth birthday was approaching and I needed more challenges in my life while I was still fit enough to tackle them. I was considering what my options might be for change, for an adventure I suppose, when my job in community education provided me with an opportunity to go on a brief study tour to Cuba. The trip was inspiring. I visited women's organisations, grassroots education projects, health centres and attended on-site classes for workers in tobacco factories. The energy of the people, their determination to make the best of what little they had was inspiring. The report I wrote on my return featured photos of billboards on Havana roadsides that carried the slogan "We do more with less" (*Hacemos más con menos*).

At the end of my trip I called into the offices of *Granma International* not far from Revolution Square in Havana. The cousin of an acquaintance from Belfast had asked me to deliver a couple of letters to an ex-girlfriend of his, a Cuban who worked there as a secretary. While I waited in the English translation department for the secretary to appear, I chatted to Liz, the departmental head. She was keen to know why I'd come to Cuba and what I thought of the country. When I explained just how positive an impression I would be taking away with me, she inquired nonchalantly whether I'd like to spend a year or so living and working in Havana. "I'd love to," I replied immediately, and I meant it.

That afternoon I did a Spanish-English translation test for Liz and she promised to phone with the results. It took her three days to call and when she did, it was with an offer of a post in her department. Those four words, "When can you start?" changed the course of my life. When I accepted I felt I was stepping off the edge of a cliff, like I was freefalling. I was elated and intimidated at the same time. A commitment of this magnitude, to a life on an island that was thousands of kilometres from my home in Ireland, would certainly be the most formidable challenge I had ever faced. I was not deluded about the enormity of this change, and the difficulty I would face in making it alone. So why did I go?

Undoubtedly, the energy and the appetite for life of the Cuban people was a key factor influencing my decision. On that study trip I found their self confidence, their vibrancy, uplifting and contagious. It contrasted with the heaviness that was dragging the peace process back home into one quagmire after another. It also gave me an antidote to the heaviness of the depression I had been struggling to emerge from for months. During those three weeks in Havana, I discovered that I could open my eyes in the morning and think of the day ahead with a feeling that wasn't dark dread, and I wanted to hold on to it.

The study trip, and then Liz's offer of work, came at a time when I was drifting, when a gap had opened up in my life that I wasn't sure how to fill. The offer of work at *Granma International* gave me direction and filled that gap. It also gave me a chance to address the regrets I had about missed opportunities in Nicaragua. I'd perhaps retreated too quickly on that occasion, allowing myself to be defeated too easily. Cuba was not Nicaragua. There was poverty, yes, but not the misery I'd witnessed in Nicaragua. There was a blockade, but no war. Standards were higher in education and health. The country was much more developed and I was confident I could cope with the heat and deprivation this time round. Maybe this was an opportunity to undertake a journey of atonement.

A further factor influencing my decision was that although I hadn't been politically active since my return from Nicaragua, my sympathies had remained broadly unchanged over the years. I regarded myself as a democratic socialist, so naturally I had a keen interest in the Cuban revolution. That interest tended toward support, particularly in the light of my opposition to the long-standing U.S. blockade of the island. During the three weeks I spent there on the study tour, I began to see the effects of the blockade, particularly on the supplies of medicine and raw materials and what the consequences were for the population. Living and working in Cuba would be an education in what life was like for people born into a society governed by Fidel Castro, possibly the most controversial political leader of the 20th century. There would never again be this unique set of historic circumstances and that this was an opportunity to satisfy my curiosity about a country that featured so significantly in global politics.

A further five months were to pass before I finally left Belfast bound for Cuba with sixty kilos of luggage. During that time there were a number of hurdles to clear before I could be confident that I really would be working in Havana. Renting my house out and giving up my job were the most difficult. But the most frustrating was getting the work visa issued by the Cuban embassy in London. There were times when it seemed that communication between the embassy and *Granma International* had broken down altogether. Crucial emails and documents were either not forthcoming or not being requested by one side or the other. The delay and periods of silence were very stressful. I was volunteering my services and consequently felt that some gratitude would be shown. Although I wasn't expecting a red carpet, I did believe that bureaucratic procedures might be expedited for volunteers. That belief was the first of many mistakes I was to make. As it was, I had to extend my time frame for arrival on the island and I landed in Havana in November 1999, a couple of months later than I had initially planned.

If I arrived later in Cuba than planned, I left the island much, much later than I had envisaged. For the first year I worked as a translator in *Granma* and thereafter I survived by doing a series of jobs, whatever I could find to earn dollars. I earned a living as a freelance translator and journalist, a tour leader for the U.S. company Global Exchange, and also a teacher. Thanks to my European newspaper editor I managed to obtain a residence permit as a member of the Foreign Press Corps. Each year he loyally provided the necessary documents which the Ministry of Foreign Affairs (MINREX) in Havana required. In reality, I did very little journalism; my main sources of income came from Global Exchange and from translations about tourism on the island.

In 2005 I left Havana to live and work in Madrid. It was only after I returned to Ireland in 2007 that I began to consider writing about my experiences in Cuba. Choosing what to include and what to omit from the narrative was the first of many difficult decisions I had to make. In the end, the guiding principle was to write about what sparkled amongst my memories and what I believe contributes to a general representation, a portrait, of what it was like to live in Cuba for me and for the people who feature in these pages.

Shortly before I began writing, I travelled back to Havana for a visit. It became clear to me then that in the five years since I had been away life on the island had undergone significant changes. The most significant one being that Fidel Castro was no longer president, Commander-in-Chief of the Revolution, and First Secretary of the Communist Party. He had been forced to resign from his leadership positions on account of illness and old age. The change in leader from Fidel to his brother Raúl has been followed by a number of new economic measures - implemented to address a growing economic and social crisis - that have impacted upon the life of the population in a way that was unimaginable while I was living in Havana. The island's timelessness, once a much-remarked-upon feature, is vanishing. It is safe, but arguably sad, to predict that the "outside world" will gain a foothold, and maybe even a stranglehold, on a society condemned to half a century of solitude. It is a society which will not, as Gabriel García Marquéz wrote, "have a second opportunity on earth".[1]

My book is an account of what it was like as an Irishwoman to live in that society.

---

[1] One Hundred Years of Solitude. Gabriel García Márquez.

CHAPTER 1

Life At Granma

I've been offered a job as a translator on the staff of the English language department at *Granma International* in Havana. It is a one-year position in a weekly newspaper which is directly responsible to the Central Committee of the Communist Party. After only a few moments' hesitation I accept. I'm in my late thirties and I know that I may never get such an opportunity again. I may not even want it. For now though, I do. I really do. Living and working in Cuba is guaranteed to transform the dull routine that my life has fallen into under these dreary Irish skies. But I don't delude myself that no matter how desperate I am for change, leaving my home, my job and my friends is a huge challenge. I feel like I'm stepping off the edge of a cliff.

I am still free-falling as I sit on the crowded Iberia flight bound for Havana on 12 November, 1999. I've been travelling since early morning - Belfast, London and then Madrid. By late afternoon I'm exhausted, and I still haven't left Europe. Mercifully, the flight departs according to schedule and now we're somewhere in the region of the Azores. Many of the other passengers are Spanish journalists who are attending the 7th Ibero-American summit, due to start a couple of days after my arrival in Cuba. I cast my eye around wistfully, slightly envious of these people who will be comfortably back home in ten days' time. I will not. The thought of having no return date is intimidating. As from tonight I will be lodging at the hotel of the Communist Party Central Committee, in Havana, where I am to stay until an apartment has been allocated to me. I'm not at all sanguine about the quality of my accommodation and wonder how quickly I will be able to procure cockroach poison. I didn't pack any and now I regret it. I have a fear of cockroaches, which I know I'll have to confront soon if I want to prevent it becoming a phobia.

A couple of hours after our departure, I squeeze past a sleeping fellow passenger into the aisle and head for the toilets, more out of a need to break the tedium than to relieve myself. As I'm fastening my belt and rearranging my shirt there is a heavy thump against the door, followed by another. Typical Spanish, I mutter to myself, no patience or consideration.

"*Un momento, POR FAVOR.*"

This is the first Spanish I've spoken in months and my voice sounds shrill.

I hurry despite my resolve not to. Setting my features into a fierce glare, I tug at the door but it won't open. It's jammed, and I tug again. A voice on the other side speaks to me in English.

"He's had a heart attack. Please don't come out."

Ignoring the instruction, I give the door an almighty shove and it opens partially, just enough for me to see a man has collapsed. He is apparently unconscious, face up, and two men are bending over him, raising his legs. There is a public appeal for a medical doctor. Trapped in the loo, with the door ajar, I've become an unwilling voyeur to what I fear is a death. His complexion is ashen and he isn't responding to the entreaties of either of his fellow passengers. I groan silently and selfishly. I don't want the flight to turn around and land in Madrid. I'm feeling wretched, utterly exhausted. I just want to land, to go to bed; I want this journey to be over, not to be protracted.

Two doctors converge on the scene. There is a swift diagnosis, and it's high blood pressure, not a heart attack. So we continue onward to Havana. No further drama takes place for another couple of hours. Then there is a fire on board. Mid-Atlantic. A passenger has been smoking furtively in the toilet and failed to fully extinguish the evidence. In tones that do not hide her fury, our flight attendant threatens the immediate detention and prosecution of the smoker in three languages. She reminds us we are half way between two continents, with only ocean beneath us and nowhere to land. Passengers around me mutter and grumble but there is no mention of a lynching party and silence soon descends on all four hundred or so of us. Half an hour later and I'm riled once again, head up, rotating left to right and right to left, meerkat-like. A nearby passenger must have unwrapped Albanian Goat's cheese. Only something dead could be more putrid. The stench is so strong I can almost touch it. But nobody at all is eating. I sink back into my seat perplexed. Then I catch sight of a pair of trainers, casually slipped off by Mr. X on my left. I incline slightly. Yes. He's oblivious to the distress he's causing, and I'm reluctant to say anything. The journey has broken me.

Five hours later, I emerge into the crowded arrivals hall of José Martí international airport, trailing over sixty kilos of luggage behind me. I am to be met by someone from *Granma International*, but I don't know by whom. All around me families reunite amidst tears, hugs and laughter. It's a sea of faces. Then I hear my name being called and I turn to see a tall thin woman stepping over my bags to welcome me. Her name, she tells me, is Pammy. She's English and she works as a translator for *Granma*. Beside her is Greg who, judging by his accent, is American, he's another English department translator at *Granma*. I summon up the energy to utter polite greetings to both of them. An elderly mulatto steps nimbly into the circle and tells me his name is Moses, and he is the driver. He says much more but his accent is so thick that I can't grasp anything other than "Moses" and "chauffeur." In response to my silence, all three smile awkwardly and usher me in the direction of the exit.

Pammy is lanky, made lankier by her big hair, big aubergine hair piled high on her head, its garishness and abundance contrasting vividly with her sallow complexion and bony body. She's fifty-something and wearing a miniskirt which does nothing to flatter her knobbly knees. Thoughts about whether the hair is real linger on in the fog of weariness, but I sharpen my focus, gather up my luggage and follow my reception committee out to the car park where we load up the boot. Five minutes later, we pull out on to the dark and deserted road to begin the journey into Havana. Every now and again I steal glances at the hair from my seat in the back of the car.

It takes us about three-quarters of an hour to get to the *hotelito del partido*, the Communist Party Central Committee hotel in the Playa district of Havana. I'm exhausted and barely able to converse beyond an exchange of a few pleasantries. None of my fellow travellers seem inclined to talk much either so we drive through the night in silence. This hush is strange for me because in Ireland I know that, as a newcomer, I would have been besieged with inquiries, such is the insatiable curiosity of the Celts. A funeral cortège ambience prevails as we drive into the suburbs of Havana, past a few late night hitchhikers, *botelleros*, who plead with the occupants of vehicles, stopped at traffic lights. I am surprised to see that a number of them are quickly accepted and happily jump aboard lorries, motorbikes and cars. I have yet to learn that these small but important acts of solidarity are a very Cuban thing, a consequence of the widespread fuel shortage that began during the worst years of the economic crisis in the early nineties.

We arrive at the *hotelito*. I feel a momentary exhilaration when I step out of the car, my skin tingles in the warm tropical air and I breathe in the thick aroma of humid earth. I'm really here. In the Caribbean. In November.

Before bidding me good night Pammy hints that I am expected at the office on the following morning, a Friday. I mumble something about being too exhausted to think about it and she looks momentarily disgruntled. Then she gathers her face into a grim smile and says she'll see me on Monday then, Agreed?"

Pammy isn't the boss. There are plenty of bosses at *Granma*, but Pammy isn't one of them…yet.

My room at the *hotelito* is small. Twin beds jammed together in one corner allow the occupant access to a built-in wardrobe over in the other. There is a small table, a stool and an *en suite* bathroom, cold water only. It is clean and adequate. The room attendant brings me a set of towels and a plastic glass. As she is leaving, she turns and informs me sweetly that overnight guests are not allowed at the *hotelito*…under no circumstances. The rule seems antiquated but it suits me since I have no plans to complicate my life by introducing a man into it. Yet, in the instant the thought arises, I know I'm deceiving myself, otherwise, would I have brought four jumbo-sized packets of condoms with me?

I roll back the 1970s-style red nylon counterpane, forage in my suitcase and unearth a pair of fresh cotton sheets. They smell of home. I smooth them onto the bumpy mattress, lie down and struggle not to allow myself to ponder on whether I've done the right thing.

Four days later and I'm feeling less shell-shocked. The weekend has been spent lounging by the pool of a nearby hotel and exploring the neighbourhood. The *hotelito* is surrounded by 1930s-style homes, a residential area for a middle class that vanished around the start of the revolution. Some are still in private hands while others have been assigned to a variety of government ministries. The houses are generally one or two storey buildings, mostly set in gardens that are overgrown with tropical vegetation. The streets around the *hotelito* are lined with exotic banyan trees, whose roots trail on to the cracked and uneven pavement. Tarzan could have swung the length of this street without touching the ground even once.

On Monday morning Moses arrives in the "company car" to collect me. He's with Jurgen, from the German department, and Octavio Fuster, *Granma*'s top man. Fuster, my new boss, is a wiry mulatto with a scarlet birthmark covering one side of his shiny bald head. The journey takes around twenty minutes but after five there's silence in the car. My upbeat chatter and friendly overtures are met with monosyllabic responses and soon I have the impression that I'm talking to myself, so I shut up. A funereal hush descends and remains with us until we drive past the immensity of the José Martí monument on Revolution Square and reach the offices. There is a power cut, so we walk past the elevator shaft and begin the seven floor ascent. On the sixth, I gasp for air and immediately wish I hadn't, the toilets must be out of order too for the acidic stench makes me gag.

Granma has five departments − Spanish, English, French, Portuguese and German, all on the seventh floor. Each is located in a room off a long grey corridor, at the beginning of which is the chief's office. Halfway down the corridor on the right is a large sign: "No admission. Authorised Personnel Only." This is the Internet room. Farther down the corridor, on the same side, is the door of the English department. I'm here with Pammy, Greg, José and Liz, the boss, who's American. Soon I'm stationed at my computer translating my first article into English, a report detailing the latest statistics for the sugar cane harvest. I sit facing the wall; in fact all of us in the department face our respective walls, or piece of wall, Zen Buddhist style. Nobody has positioned their desk against the large window, which is overlooked on the left by the sombre granite building that serves as headquarters for the Central Committee. On the right is the Armed Forces command centre. On my first day I see this arrangement of furniture as odd; within weeks though, I come to prefer it.

This way I don't have to look at the boredom, fatigue and utter despair on my colleagues' faces.

At lunchtime Pammy and Greg take me down to the works canteen, located in the basement of the building. José, the only Cuban in the office, doesn't join us, and neither does Liz. Greg sniggers as we stand in the queue waiting to be served from a hatch.

"*Be prepared*," he warns.

Pammy says nothing.

An upturned palm appears through the hatch in front of me. Pammy nudges me and I hand over my token, which entitles me to my subsidised meal. An aluminium tray, prison style, is pushed out toward me.

"*Por favor,* I'm vegetarian."

Greg sniggers again. Pammy shushes us. So I shush and reach for my tray.

Grey, the colour grey, is what I'm faced with when I look at the rations that have been served to me. I'm told it is boiled plantain, boiled tarot, and rice pudding. All of it is grey. Even the scraps of meat that accompany this mush have assumed an identical hue of grey. Gingerly, I prod it. If grey could be a taste, it would be insipid and if it had a texture it would be gelatinous. I peck at it and my suspicions are confirmed: the food is both insipid and gelatinous. I think I see singed hairs growing out of the meat as I pass it over to Pammy, who is not vegetarian. I'm repulsed. I'm only nibbling at the meal out of politeness because I find it completely inedible. This is my introduction to canteen food in *Granma* and subsequent experience has given me no reason to believe that it is either better or worse than what is served in other workplaces throughout Havana. Indeed, I see that the surrounding tables are full, so I presume my co-workers, comrades rather, must be used to it. Looking around at them, I feel ungrateful and petulant. The meal is, after all, subsidised. It's a goodwill gesture. It doesn't seem like that, though, as I look down at my plate. The food could have been cooked better and more imaginatively at no extra cost. Once upon a time those plantains and that tarot were the palatable ingredients of a potentially appetising meal.

But now that they've fallen into the hands of cooks and kitchen staff who are indifferent and apathetic, they've become an abomination. When I get back to my desk I hastily consult my dictionary for my first new word in my new job, and test it out on José. He understands my dictionary term but tells me that in Cuba people tend to call swill *sancoche*. I don't tell him why I want to be able to say swill in Cuban Spanish.

It's my first day and I'm as yet unaware that my new workplace is run as an integral part of the hierarchical and quasi-military structure of the Party. This is about to change. I'm battling with some of the more challenging vocabulary in my first few articles when Octavio storms into the office, startling me. He's apoplectic, raging about poor staff attendance, thumping the table and spittle is flying everywhere. Liz swings round in her chair to face him; she listens to his tirade, makes sympathetic noises and undertakes to ensure that the English language department staff will not be culpable on that score. Octavio doesn't look convinced. He glares at me and then stomps out, still bellicose. I'm stunned by the outburst. This is in stark contrast to the easy-going ambience of the west Belfast community group I have just left. When he's gone, in an attempt to break the tense silence, I make an intentionally light-hearted remark about him not taking any prisoners. Nobody laughs. What I don't know is that he is furious with me for not starting work the previous Friday, and that outbursts of this nature are a frequent occurrence, although I'm already beginning to suspect that there is no "craic" (banter) at all in these offices.

As the days and weeks go by I learn that absenteeism is a major problem in *Granma*, and elsewhere in Cuba. The authorities endeavour to combat it via a system of *estímulos,* or bonuses, for attendance and performance that consist of modest financial rewards, either in Cuban pesos or in hard currency (dollars). There are also the twice yearly *jabas*, plastic carrier bags filled with items such as razor blades, toothpaste, deodorant, detergent and some other toiletries. Cubans look forward to, and delight in receiving, their *jaba* since it is, for the majority, the only access they have to such "luxury" goods. Despite being virtually negligible in terms of monetary value, the *jabas* make a significant difference to the quality of life for the average employee, and management know this, which is why sanctions usually entail withholding the cash bonus or *jaba*, or both. When an entire workforce is punished this way morale plummets and resentment runs high, much higher than usual.

Ocatvio's management style intimidates me and I soon learn that Liz applies similar tactics in the English department. She looks like a woman with serious issues, and indeed she is. Most of her hair has fallen out due to stress, and she's grossly overweight. Her behaviour is volatile; she easily flies off the handle and reprimands her staff constantly, irrespective of how accurately or quickly we work. From very early on my translations are singled out for criticism, which she delivers in nervous high pitched tones, tones that make me think she is on the verge of hysterical laughter, and she may well be.

"Revolution is spelt with a capital R."

"But it is," I protest, pointing to the big R.

"That's just the start of the sentence. I mean always, every single time it appears in our newspaper, it is to be spelt with a capital R."

"Even in the middle of a sentence? Like God, you mean?"

She scowls, unsure of whether I am ridiculing her or the Revolution.

Liz is burnt out both emotionally and intellectually, damaged by years of mind-numbingly tedious work and the multiple infidelities of her musician husband. She makes no attempt to conceal her marital problems from the four of us. As the weeks go by, the number and intensity of the rows with her husband goes up. Today is not untypical. There has been a heated exchange by telephone during which Liz has shouted, threatened, pleaded and wept. Twice she has slammed the receiver down and swept out of the office sobbing uncontrollably. Now she's back, perched ponderously on her swivel chair, hammering at the keyboard. The phone rings, and she's shrieking again. Jurgen, who is in an adjacent office, pops his head around the door to see what's happening. I see his lips moving but I can't hear what he's saying because Liz's screams into the receiver are ear-splittingly loud. She's unleashing her fury at her husband as if there was nobody else around. She's completely uninhibited. Jurgen looks at me, rolls his eyes and shrugs his shoulders. Just then there's a deafening crash. Liz has hurled the phone against the wall. Jurgen backs out of the room swiftly and closes the door. Nobody moves. José, Greg, Pammy and I continue to work at our computers in silence. Liz is weeping loudly but no one approaches her. I'm thinking that this is a madhouse and that if I ever record these events in a book, nobody will believe me.

There are numerous days, even weeks on end, when Liz does not report for work. Sometimes she phones to say that she'll be on sick leave due to personal problems, and sometimes she simply doesn't bother phoning. After an absence, even an extended absence, she breezes into the office and takes up her position with her back to us, as if she had not been away from work at all. The silence is tense. On these days we know better than to enquire how she has been or even to initiate a conversation with her about her "disappearance". It's hard not to feel a deep and bitter resentment when each of her absences results in a twenty-five per cent increase in the workload for each of us; this is the consequence when one person in a team of four is absent.

One afternoon in late February Liz arrives late. We haven't seen her for three days. Around three o'clock, the door of the office opens abruptly and dramatically. Pammy, Greg, José and I look up. Liz's vast bulk occupies the frame. She is immobile, apparition-like and we stare transfixed. Her face is blackened, as if she'd been caught in an explosion. She smiles sheepishly and the whiteness of her teeth and eyes contrast comically with the grime on her face.

"I've had a flat tyre."

And then she holds up both hands for emphasis. They too are streaked with oil.

"Now, I'm going to have to go home to clean up."

We don't see her until the following Monday.

José is the only Cuban in the English department. He's been working at *Granma* for decades, and according to Greg, he's Octavio's personal translator. When I ask what this involves, he tells me that José translates into English the texts that are beyond our chief's grasp of the language. Initially, I see José's behaviour as odd. Months go by without him exchanging anything more than a couple of sentences with the rest of us. He is furtive, beetling in and out of the office, apparently busy. But he's not, for I often see him idling in the long grey corridor or staring out of the only window on the floor which doesn't frame the Central Committee building. Greg boasts that he's had a few interesting conversations with José, enough to prove that he's still sane and connected to reality, so one afternoon, when the office is empty, I decide to test him and surprisingly, maybe because we are alone, he opens up to me. I discover that José paints in his spare time, that he cares for his ailing mother and that for several years he used to walk eight kilometres in the morning and then again in the evening, devoting almost five hours of his day to the task of getting to and from work. Fuel was scarce and transport was irregular and unreliable, and Octavio needed his services, he adds. I ask José how he has coped with life at *Granma* for so long. His expression dulls over and he mutters something about retiring soon. Then he turns to face the wall. I'm sorry I asked the question. Now I can't avoid thinking of José as a casualty.

Within the first couple of weeks of my year at *Granma*, a name that I shall never forget, *Elián,* comes to dominate our life at the office. Much of my work involves translating information related to Elián González, a six-year-old Cuban boy rescued off the coast of Florida after his mother, and many of those with her, drowned in their attempt to reach the US illegally on a raft. His uncle Lázaro immediately claims custody of the child in Miami and refuses to return him to his father, Juan Miguel, in Cuba. A legal battle ensues, involving both sides of Elián's family, the Cuban government and the U.S. authorities. There is widespread international publicity surrounding the case, and it is treated as priority news throughout the island. The number of articles I translate about the case for the newspaper seems to double and treble as the Cuban government steps up its campaign to have the child returned to the island. We are required to do seemingly endless hours of voluntary work in order to keep abreast of developments.

There are late nights when I have to type my own translations, unchecked, directly on to the digital version of *Granma International*, meaning they go immediately online. I'm anxious that due to exhaustion, I'll make a mistake that could have serious consequences. Omitting a word like "no" from an article, making a negative into an affirmative, could cause a diplomatic incident. It's like walking a tightrope. I reach the limit of my endurance. I can't bear to read the name Elián González any longer. When I have the choice I translate banal texts on tourism statistics, health care provision and worker-of-the month features. Anything but Elián González. I'm not the only one who feels this way. A leading news presenter, Laritza Ulloa, suddenly vanishes from our screens after she makes a disparaging remark about the saturation coverage of the Elián case, unaware that she was still being broadcast on live television.

Throughout the seven months of the campaign, rallies are held in Havana and in the provinces. Tens, and often hundreds, of thousands leave their work to march past the US Interests Section in the capital, in protest at the abduction of Elián. Fidel is frequently at the head of these weekly marches. Workplaces close early and transport, including public transport, is commandeered to maximise attendance at these monster events. When this happens the only way to get home is by bicycle or taxi. I'm also concerned about how these frequent stoppages will affect the fragile national economy, and I'm not the only one. But dissent is muted or whispered in off-the-record comments. I don't march with the others because I know that if I do, I'll have to return to my desk after the rally and catch up on the work I've missed. It's a sacrifice I'm not prepared to make. My Cuban colleagues have no choice but to attend...and they unfailingly do so because lists of names are read out by heads of department and ticked off accordingly, or not, when contingents gather at the start of each protest march.

In the street one evening, after a monster rally, I hear some children laughing and singing in rhyme,

"Elián mi amigo, llévame contigo." (Elián my friend, take me with you.)

In the week leading up to International Women's Day an incident occurs that illustrates the need for greater democracy at shop floor level in *Granma*. It's mid-afternoon and I'm working at my computer. Edith sidles in with a new batch of texts to be translated. She's in and out of the office in a flash, suspiciously quickly, so I whip round in my chair to look at what she has left us. Instead of the usual three or four pages there is a wad of material, a series of articles written to commemorate the occasion. In seconds our workload has increased by fifty per cent and yet we can barely keep up with the demands being made on us. No one has consulted us about this. Liz is absent and the others shrug their shoulders when I protest that too much is being asked of us.

I take the wad into the Portuguese department, where there are only three translators, all Cuban, who struggle to cope with the workload. They look at me aghast. My outspokenness has frightened them and they tell me I'm wasting my time complaining. In the French department the reception is different. Didier is delighted that somebody else on *Granma* staff is defending workers' rights to negotiate the workload. We agree that we have to request a meeting with management to protest. This is not "sacrifice" for the revolution, as the leadership like to call it, it is exploitation. Carried away by the mood of rebellion, I suggest jokingly that we organise a strike for greater democracy in the workplace. I don't see Natasha, the chief's Russian wife, standing behind the door until the words are out of my mouth.

A meeting is arranged between Octavio and the heads of department for Friday morning at 9.00 am sharp. I'm attending an outpatient appointment for an ear infection at a nearby hospital and arrive shortly after 11.00 am. Didier emerges from his office as I'm walking down the corridor toward the English department and demands to know where I've been. He accuses me of backing out. I stare at him in surprise. Octavio, he says, emerged from his office in a fury just before nine ordering all "strikers" to report to him immediately. He does not take "insubordination" lightly. Pammy, Liz, and Jurgen were absent so he and Angel, from the Portuguese department, had to face the chief on their own. In the end, to his credit, Octavio agreed that the demands being placed on translators were excessive, for this week only. It was a short-term victory. Nothing else could be expected, Didier stresses, with a look that said I had betrayed him.

Monthly staff meetings are held at *Granma* as a forum for airing views and resolving grievances. Senior management attends, as do Party officials and trade union representatives. My initial enthusiasm turns quickly to cynicism as I witness what seems to be a façade. An agenda is covered and procedures are followed mechanically. Nobody raises issues of any substance and no complaints are voiced. The meetings are scheduled for late on Friday afternoons, when a mood of weariness generally prevails, a mood which turns to irritation when Jurgen takes the opportunity to address management, as he is doing today, to expound a long-standing grievance in monotones. At least a dozen pairs of eyes glare hostilely in his direction, and they're all from his co-workers. Some glance at their wristwatches, then again at Jurgen, and yawn pointedly. It is clear that they want to go home and that they've heard this before; after all Jurgen has been working at *Granma* for seven years, and little, if anything, has changed.

Just before five o'clock, I head back to my desk to finish the text I was translating before leaving. I've no plans for the weekend but I'm thinking about it when I open the door of the department and see Liz at her desk. Immediately I feel a substantial drop in the temperature. The air conditioning is on full again. It's a Russian device that hums angrily in the corner. This is Liz's way of punishing us. She switches it on full and leaves it like that, at refrigeration temperature. As soon as she walks out of the office, we leap up and turn it down, hoping she won't notice. But Liz always does. When she comes back into the room she lifts her nose in the air, apparently sensing that something is amiss, tuts, strides over to the device and turns it up again. It's a silent, protracted, low-intensity war. Already I've fallen ill with flu three times since my arrival in Havana so I reach for my alpaca wool cardigan. It's May, this is Cuba, and I'm cold.

CHAPTER 2

Now What Do I Do?

Granma has finally allocated me my own apartment, five months after my arrival in Havana. I know I should be grateful for free accommodation but now that I've seen it my excitement and impatience have evaporated. Dreary, unappealing, and alienating, it is a place I fear will deepen my loneliness. I don't want to live there, I want to stay on in the *hotelito*, but I have no choice in the matter. This apartment in a block of flats on Avenida de mayo is going to be my official abode for as long as I am on the newspaper staff, so I set about making it habitable, which is why I'm cleaning and fumigating every square centimetre of the place.

Elisa is coming to help me. She is my first real friend and confidant in Cuba. I meet her soon after arriving at *Granma,* when she comes into the English department one morning and whispers that she sells *cocitos*. Cuban Spanish is significantly different from the Spanish I had picked up during my time in Barcelona so I have no idea what she's talking about. After she leaves, I turn to Pammy, who tells me that I'll like the *cocitos*, they're delicious little cakes made from fresh coconut.

"Go and see her in her office at the end of the corridor. But be discreet, very discrete."

The coconut cakes are loaded with sugar, too much for me. Nevertheless, I return every day to Elisa's office and buy one or two ... discretely because I like her and want to help her out, if I can, with her finances. When there is no coconut available she brings in a couple of flasks of coffee and sells delicious tiny espressos for 1 peso, about 5 cents. It's absolutely forbidden to engage in business or any profit-making activities in the workplace at the risk of disciplinary action. Yet it's a risk Elisa is prepared to take because she has two children and cannot support them on her monthly salary of less than $20.00 USD – she is a print engineer at the newspaper. She supplements her income by selling *cocitos* and also by working on the side as a seamstress from her home at weekends. Thanks to the *cocitos* and her skills with the sewing machine, Elisa and her daughters survive ... just about. Some societies might applaud her entrepreneurial initiative, but in Cuba it is different; here it arouses suspicion of her trust in the Revolution to provide for her and her family.

Elisa is of African descent and originally from the east of Cuba, where her ancestors would have been forced to work as slaves on the sugar plantations. She is what the *habaneros* like to call an Oriental, and she is still referred to as such, even though she's been living in Havana for half her life and rarely goes back east to see her family. A number of years have elapsed since she last saw her mother and sisters but the journey is costly, time-consuming and too arduous for her to undertake with her children. Getting a train or bus ticket in Cuban pesos requires stoicism for the all-night queues; if you have the extra cash there is always the option of paying a volunteer to stand in line for you. Even tourists and those willing and able to pay in hard currency – who are in the fast-track queue – may find the whole business of buying rail and bus tickets very time consuming.

Elisa's entire professional career has been spent at *Granma*. She joined the newspaper shortly after graduating with a degree in print engineering from a Russian-speaking university in the Ukraine. Those six years in the former Soviet Union weren't a happy time for her, mainly because she couldn't adapt to the freezing temperatures and found the people difficult to relate to. But she's glad she went, and is proud of herself for having accepted the challenge of learning Russian and completing her education in the language. One afternoon she turns to me and says,

"There are some things you have to be very grateful to this Revolution for. I'm a poor black woman from a rural area and if I speak Russian and work as a professional it's thanks to the Revolution. Where else in the world could I have had such an opportunity?"

Of all the Cubans that I've talked to so far, Elisa has the most balanced attitude toward the government. She doesn't want to leave her position at *Granma* because she feels she has a debt to pay, firstly for sponsoring her education 100 per cent, and secondly for social welfare provision. She pulls out her ration book and explains how her family would not have enough to eat without the subsidised rice, beans, coffee, sugar and milk that it entitles her to. Jennyfer, her youngest, receives a litre of milk daily at minimal cost because she is under seven years old. Apart from the milk, there is another privilege attached to being a child in Cuba. Every year Jennyfer gets a birthday cake at a special subsidised rate from the local bakery. These state birthday cakes can be seen on almost any day in the streets of Havana, often balanced precariously on someone's head or shoulder, and often when they are riding pillion on a scooter or a bicycle. They are garishly-decorated blue and white, or pink and white affairs that most Cubans seem to delight in. A generous slab of birthday cake is sometimes served with our afternoon coffee on Friday afternoons at *Granma*, but after a couple of mouthfuls I pass the rest on to José or Greg because it is sickeningly sugary, even for my sweet tooth.

A few weeks after I meet her, Elisa invites me to her home in the Cerro neighbourhood. We walk there together after work one afternoon. It takes about twenty minutes to get there but the temperatures are scorching and the humidity is so intense that we arrive drenched in sweat. The entire neighbourhood is in a state of advanced decay. Façades are crumbling, potholes scar the road surfaces, a putrid stench arises from blocked drains and, I note, there are no trees anywhere. There's a world of difference between the leafy jasmine-scented streets surrounding my *hotelito* in Playa and the rawness I encounter in El Cerro. I didn't know that afternoon that the area had something of a reputation for crime or that my apartment would be located right here.

Elisa's home is set in one of the many colonial buildings typical of the architecture in the neighbourhood. A large crack traverses the exterior, running from the lintel of the main door past the set of windows on the first floor, and up to the roof. I'm not surprised when she tells me that it has been condemned as structurally unsound. Yet in spite of the danger nobody has moved out because they've nowhere to go. We stop in the doorway momentarily, enough time for our eyes to adjust to the darkness. There was a light bulb here, once, Elisa says, but it was stolen last year and nobody has bothered to replace it, and there would be no point anyway because it would just vanish again. She guides me up the stone steps of the stairwell leading to the first floor, and we emerge, blinking, in the sunlight again. We pause briefly on a narrow landing overlooking a small square courtyard. I glance down and see a woman preparing coffee beans for roasting while a child tugs at her skirt. A man I assume to be her husband is bent over a work bench in the corner. Next to him is a pile of shoes; he is repairing them. We are just one step away from another era.

The building is probably about two hundred years old, dating back to the times when slavery was legal in Cuba. We are in what is called a multi-family dwelling. It wasn't originally designed for so many people but with the pre revolutionary chaos and the upheaval that followed in 1959 thousands of homes throughout the country were invaded by squatters. About nine families live here now, and three of them share the same landing with Elisa and their doors lie open, ready to welcome the occasional breeze which might lift the inhabitants from their heat-sedated torpor. Half a dozen television sets are switched on, giving a stereophonic effect to the late afternoon children's programmes. A small hairless dog lifts its head drowsily as we step over and drops it again, apparently uninterested in my presence.

We continue along the landing to a large cage-like structure, secured with a padlock, which frames the entrance to Elisa's home. Behind it is a heavy and battered ancient wooden door, probably fitted in the pre-revolution era, and possibly even in the previous century. She unlocks it and we step inside, into the space she shares with her daughters. I'm appalled. There's no kind way to describe it other than as a hovel. Her home is one room and it serves as a kitchen, living room, and bedroom for the three of them. In the corner there is a walled space, about the size of a telephone box, and this is the bathroom. There is no bath or shower, just a discoloured toilet and a tiny metal sink. Elisa tells me that there is no running water either, so "showers" are in fact water scooped from a bucket, which is tipped over the head and runs down into a hole in the floor. I glance around and see that the place is clean, and it is homely. Elisa clearly cares about this tiny space and I feel ashamed for finding it so deplorable.

Elisa introduces me to her two daughters, who are eleven and six years old. Both girls are much whiter than their mother, particularly the youngest one. The question mark must have been discernible on my face and Elisa doesn't hesitate to clarify.

"I was mindful when I chose white men for their fathers. *Mulattos* have better chances in life than blacks, they're more beautiful and that counts for a lot in this country."

She laughs and adds: "You could say that I'm *whitening* our family."

I don't know what to say to this, but I do agree that the girls are very pretty indeed. I'm curious about where they were when we came in because I didn't see them.

They've descended a very steep ladder that leads to a hole in the ceiling. Elisa laughs when I look up.

"That's a *barbacoa*. Do you know what *barbacoa* is?"

Certainly not a barbeque.

I admit that I don't, so she leads me over to the ladders and we climb into an improvised room, a construction only possible in colonial style buildings, where there are high ceilings. The makeshift ceiling/floor divides one room into two, horizontally, in order to create double the amount of living space. I climb off the ladder and step on to a floor made of rough planks laid slightly unevenly. It's stifling up here.

"I only wanted you to see it. Don't hang around up here, it's not very safe. The roof could collapse at any time, which is why all three of us sleep in the living room."

The girls watch television while Elisa prepares dinner. She knows I'm vegetarian and jokes that I'm welcome to come any time for dinner. There's rarely any meat in the house anyway.

Within an hour the table is spread with a colourful meal of fried plantain, black bean stew, rice, a green salad and boiled eggs. Just as we are about to start eating Elisa sinks her head in her hands and begins to weep silently. Her eldest daughter rises and hugs her. I feel uncomfortable and ask if I can help. She tells me that the sight of so much food, this banquet, is overwhelming, hard to believe.

"You can't understand my reaction when I see this quantity of food in front of me because you haven't had to suffer the hunger that we've suffered. You don't know what it's like to fear that you might starve to death."

She tells me about the terrifying weeks and months – and years too – that followed the collapse of the Soviet

Union at the start of the nineties, when the Cuban economy went into freefall. Almost overnight life on the island was transformed for the worst by chronic shortages of fuel, raw materials and –inevitably – food.

"Until then, we never fully appreciated the way in which the socialist bloc kept us afloat with shiploads of subsidised oil, and that was only part of the help they gave us. When it was gone we had nothing and we were totally unprepared for it. The hardest part was watching big strong men, your family and friends, fade away as the kilos dropped off them. Beefy men were turned into scarecrows in a matter of weeks."

Since fuel was so scarce, what produce there was could not be transported from the countryside to the city and it began to rot in the fields. One day, Elisa explains, out of desperation she took a train, the first train she could find that was leaving Havana, and got off in the countryside. She was struck to see scores of other passengers doing the same. They all got off the train, walked into the nearest field and started tugging vegetables out of the soil.

"It was a heartrending sight. Stick-thin men and women were roaming the fields that day looking for something to eat. I'll never forget and I don't think I'll ever get over the trauma of hunger and that's why I have this terrible anxiety around food now."

I wasn't witness to that scene, but the image she evoked has remained with me always, reminding me of haunting sketches I've seen of the 19th century Irish famine. Her story conveys, better than the most broad-ranging statistics or academic lecture, the economic and social catastrophe that ensued when aid and subsidies from the Soviet Union and Eastern Europe ended so abruptly.

After that night I become a frequent visitor to Elisa's home and soon come to rely on her advice and companionship. Without her I would be at a loss as to how to deal with the practical problems of moving into my new flat, primarily the cockroach plague which I feel powerless to confront. I've only been here for a couple of days and I'm overwhelmed by what has to be done to make the place habitable. I miss my tiny room at the *hotelito* and the comfort of my life there.

My new address is halfway down *Avenida 20 de mayo*, about a fifteen minute walk from the *Granma* offices. It's on the fourth floor of a 1970s building that is eleven storeys high and houses around a hundred or so such flats. Beside it is the base where the long distance Aspro buses park at night.

I have the micro brigades to thank for my new home. Micro brigades are teams of volunteers who are allocated apartments in exchange for their labour, for investing time and energy in a residential construction project. This was a nationwide scheme set up to confront the chronic shortage of housing on the island in the 1970s. In this case, the volunteers were *Granma* workers – reporters, office staff, cleaners, technicians and management – who spent between one or two years working on the construction site and acquired a home at a very modest price as part of the deal. It's easy to spot micro-brigade accommodation; the daunting Soviet style pragmatic architecture of these buildings make them an anomaly in the tropical cityscape. There are a lot of them in Havana and, indeed, throughout Cuba, although subsequent building projects are generally more pleasing aesthetically.

My flat has no personality. It is a vast grey space, with grey floors, greying walls, and louvre-style aluminium slats set in glassless windows. Furniture is minimal, and what there is, tends to be rickety and rotten. There's a modest-sized kitchen, a bathroom and two bedrooms. The emptiness of the larger of the two echoes in a way that reminds me of an abandoned warehouse, so I choose to sleep in the smaller. At night the fumes of long-distance buses pulling into the depot beneath my window filter through the louvre slats and choke me.

For the first couple of nights I leave the light switched on in the corridor outside my room in the hope that it will fool the cockroaches into believing it's daytime and too dangerous to emerge. When I wake with the urge to use the toilet I purposefully shuffle, cough and stamp around in my room, sending out warning signals. But the cockroaches only rarely scuttle off when they sense my presence, their tactic is to freeze, to remain motionless wherever they happen to be on their prowls while their antennae twitch nervously, seeking the source of the disturbance. Very often they stand between me and the bathroom.

Elisa arrives on the morning of the third day and we systematically move from room to room using bleach and ammonia-based detergent. The purge is a revelation for me. For the first time in my life I see cockroach eggs, miniature kidney beans stuck to the backs of wardrobes, on the undersides of chairs and wedged in the creases of armchairs. In the bathroom we discover a particularly large black specimen living under the ridges of the toilet bowl. He won't flush away so I pour undiluted bleach directly on to him. We cover every centimetre, working late into Saturday night. Our hands are raw when we finish but I'm confident that I've won the initial battle as I gaze at a couple of dozen carcasses strewn along the corridor. Any lone survivors will be wiped out when Alberto, the fumigator, comes in the morning. I couldn't have done it on my own; battling against vermin and so much dirt would have depressed me and I say so with gratitude to Elisa.

When she leaves it's close to midnight, and that's when the fluorescent light bulb in the kitchen dies. It won't be easy to find a replacement. Elisa is bound to know where I can begin my search. I turn on late night radio, *Radio Rebelde*, and listen to requests being broadcast to Cuban medical personnel stationed in Central America. Many of these doctors and nurses are sent on overseas missions to remote parts of Nicaragua, Honduras and El Salvador, where only sporadic contact with their family back on the island is possible. I imagine the sound of the crackling, undulating, Cuban accent reaching them on long wave radio in their isolated hamlet on a volcano slope somewhere magnifies their loneliness.

Over the following weeks and months my friendship with Elisa strengthens and we share many companionable evenings at her place, not mine. I've got more than three times as much living space than she has, and it's infinitely more comfortable, yet there is no question that I still prefer to be in her home with her family. I whinge about how lonely I am in the flat, yet my friend always listens with compassion; it must be hard for her to sympathise, but she does.

Elisa could have been Irish. She has a gift for story telling and a wonderfully dark sense of humour. She laughs and asks if I want to learn about the fate of her beloved *jicotea*, her pet turtle. I scan the floor and glance over to the bathroom seeking her pet, which usually shuffles alongside the skirting, stopping now and again to sleep, before continuing its tedious circumnavigation. This is the route it has followed for seven years, the same unending journey that never leads to the sea. I can't see it anywhere.

"Where is it?"

I'm immediately fearful that she's eaten it. Only two weeks previously some Cuban friends had confessed to me how, in the absence of meat, they once added the family turtle to the chick pea stew. Killing it was the hard part, they explained. Even though turtles are a family pet they still sense when there is danger and withdraw into their shell, and then they won't come out; it's like a cast-iron fortress.

I was reluctant to ask this question, but felt it was expected of me.

"So what did you do?"

"*Le dimos candela.*"

My peninsular Spanish wasn't up to this *candela* word, so I had to ask. Mimicking the dreadful deed, my friends held up an imaginary *jicotea*, produced a lighter, flicked it on and put the flame to where the tail of the unfortunate creature would be.

"It can't stand the heat so it peeps out to see what's happening and BAM, the knife comes down and the head is off."

I recoiled.

But this is not the fate of Elisa's pet. The previous evening while she was working at her sewing machine a sudden movement by the door caught her eye. It was a rat that had slipped in through the bars of "the cage." While she was reaching for her shoes the rat snapped off the turtle's head. It had been dozing and probably never felt a thing she hoped.

"My poor *jicotea*. Decapitated. The rat escaped through the door with the head in its mouth."

Just then Joana sniggers.

"Jennyfer thinks it ran away."

I stomp loudly and cough repeatedly as I step out of "the cage" to feel my way down the stairwell and out into the night.

A few weeks later I arrive on a Saturday morning with my bag of weekly laundry. I'm fed up scrubbing with a nail brush and have decided it's easier to walk to Elisa's and feed my clothes into her ancient Soviet twin tub, running the risk that it might chew up my knickers in the process. When I arrive, Elisa has already hauled the twin tub into the centre of the living room and Joana is filling it with buckets of water. They've been waiting for me because I'd promised to buy the detergent for them in my local supermarket. At the moment only hard currency soap powder is available; the alternative is a block of yellowish-grey scrubbing soap. I hand over my load and Elisa tips it into the tub. She presses a switch and the machine rumbles into action, creating a frothy whirlpool from the ingredients it has just been fed. Once the wash has finished, Elisa rinses the clothes by hand and hangs them out to dry along a line strung from the ornate iron railings that frame the courtyard. On the days when washing is out there Joana sits by the door, doing her homework and keeping an eye out to prevent their clothes being snatched from the line.

This morning we don't get a chance to rinse because the rumbling suddenly ceases and the whirlpool halts. Immediately we look up, and ... yes the lights have gone out. It's another power cut. We groan. Downstairs the coffee grinder splutters momentarily and halts. A second later, the silence is broken when a woman screeches:

*C-o-j-o-n-e-s. ¿Ahora qué hago? (*Balls. Now what do I do?)

Elisa is more discreet and limits herself to an inoffensive

Ay mi madre (something like "Oh Mummy").

This power cut is earlier than usual. We had been hoping to get all the washing on the line by midday, but now we are going to have to leave it in the tub. If we try to finish the laundry by hand we risk ending up with no water at all. Elisa's home is unlike most others in Cuba in that she is not fortunate enough to have the option of mains water pumping water into a spacious reserve tank on the roof. Her emergency supply is in two large plastic barrels in the corner of her living room, which she assiduously fills using a hosepipe connected to the tap in the kitchen. The barrels are all she has to rely on during the numerous hours that mains water is not available. Without electricity, no water is pumped into the building; so we are forced to halt the work until the power is switched on again. It could take hours for that to happen and until then nothing can be done except sit by the window where there is light and an occasional breeze, and wait. Elisa tells me that last month an émigré returned home from Miami on a visit, his first since he'd left the island in the early nineties. It was rumoured that he paid a bribe to admin staff at the local electricity authority office to ensure there were no power cuts during his two-week stay.

"And there weren't. None at all. Imagine that! Ten years ago this guy and his family left under a hail of abuse. A crowd organised by the CDR gathered outside his home and hurled insults at them in what was called an act of repudiation. They were accused of cowardice and treason, just like all the others who couldn't cope with the misery of living in a country where the economy had gone into freefall. Now he returns from Miami with wads of money, enough to fund the electricity supply for all of us, including those who called him a traitor. It's ironic."

I go home before the power supply returns because I'm expecting Alberto, the fumigator, some time after lunch. Just recently the cockroaches appear to have regrouped and have been creeping around the skirting boards in Indian file, so I fear that a second invasion is imminent. On his first visit Alberto warned me that I should have the flat treated regularly, every month, otherwise the numbers would grow again. He was right. Some nights I catch fleeting glimpses of the hideous marauders in the vicinity of the kitchen but when I advance they flit around the corner and vanish. Three nights previously I was in the living room watching

Cubavision news when movement in the corridor caught my attention.

An unusually large roach was out on early patrol, it didn't even have the courtesy to wait for total darkness, and it was advancing. I watched, mesmerised and horrified by its bulk. This was a cocksure specimen, fearless, for it wasn't even hugging the skirting. If cockroaches can swagger then this beast was swaggering, lumberjack-style, towards me. The news droned on in the background. I lifted both feet slowly as a precaution. Now it was only about six feet away. The antennae were twitching almost imperceptibly, in a way that suggested an intelligence was at work, sinisterly weighing up the situation. I coughed and the twitching became frantic but the advance continued. I grabbed a book and slammed it down on the surface of the coffee table next to me, creating powerful sound and air vibrations. The cockroach halted, reversed a few steps, did a *volte face* and raced for the front door, or rather *under* the front door. I could almost hear its armour scrape against the bottom ridge of the wood. I swore to myself, *Jesús, María y José*.

A few seconds later and I hear that word again, for the second time today,

C-o-j-o-n-e-s!

I deduce that the lumberjack must have made it into my neighbour's living room.

A couple of dull heavy thuds, and then a third, even more determined crash, suggest a messy execution. I reach for my glass of rum and upend it in a vague gesture of gratitude to my neighbour.

So I'm glad when Alberto arrives with his array of bottles and sprays. He's hot and sweaty, dangerously pink in the face because he's a redhead, one of the few Cubans who have this anomalous Celtic colouring. Freckles and white skin don't adapt well to the Caribbean sun, so he wears long sleeves and a baseball cap, even at 30º C plus and 90 per cent humidity.

Alberto is a civil engineer by profession but his main source of income comes from exterminating cockroaches. From nine to five he works on internationally-funded projects set up with the aim of restoring and preserving the colonial architecture in Old Havana. Every evening and most weekends he gets on his bike and cycles to his clients around the city who need his services in the war against vermin. I offer him a glass of cold water and some herbal tea. On his first visit Alberto tells me that I should always close the blinds if I think it is going to rain because that is when the "pilots" are likely to fly into the apartment, seeking refuge.

"Pilots?"

Pilots, he cheerfully explains, are flying cockroaches. I stare at him in disbelief.

"My poison is really only fully effective against the ones that don't have wings."

The sky is overcast right now, so I close the blinds as a precaution.

When I offered Alberto *un cafecito* on that first visit he surprised me by saying that he doesn't drink coffee or alcohol, he's vegetarian and a Buddhist. He talked to me about energy centres in the body called chakras, which I've never heard of before. Today he has come back with seven pages of elaborate drawings and explanations he has copied from a book that someone gave him years ago, a book, he says, that has changed his life.

I look down at the sheaf Alberto has just handed me, he must have devoted hours to the task. Either he has no access to a photocopier or he can't afford to use one, but he has kept his promise to give me information about chakras. When I've expressed my thanks, which is hardly enough considering the time and effort he has invested in these pages, Alberto proceeds to demonstrate an ancient Tibetan ritual saluting the morning sun which, he claims, will bring me lifelong health and happiness. It's too complicated and a tad too mystical for me to follow, but he's so earnest that I pretend to be interested anyway. In fact, I'm revelling in the bizarreness of the moment: a cockroach exterminator-civil engineer-Buddhist mystic teaching me how to salute the sun in my Havana flat.

That night I lie in bed, blinds closed, listening to the roar of the excited crowd from the nearby baseball stadium. Judging by the chants I guess that *Industriales*, the home team, is playing. Games start after sundown, when the heat is less fierce, and continue until midnight, or even later. The floodlights cast a silvery light over the bedroom, almost as if a full moon was shining directly through the louvre slats. A long-distance bus pulls into the parking area beneath my window. The engine revs repeatedly as it waits for the barrier to be lifted. The noise makes it impossible to sleep. Diesel fumes filter through into the room and irritate my throat. I promise myself that if I stay in Cuba when the contract with *Granma* runs out my next flat will be nowhere near a bus station or a baseball stadium.

CHAPTER 3

A Strategy: The Three S's

Orlando is standing in the middle of my room at the *hotelito*. He has just undone his fly and is displaying his penis. I'm not aware of this yet because I have my back to him, rooting in the depths of my wardrobe for the spare mouse. With the mouse in my hand I turn around to face him.

"At last! I've got it."

But I don't get it. I don't get why his penis is hanging out of his fly because it wasn't twenty seconds ago and neither of us has said or done anything to prompt this development.

I gape at him ... at it.

He smiles like a contented child.

This is my first experience of "exposure" in Cuba. At least, I think it's exposure, to say it was "flashing" would perhaps suggest a sort of now-you-see-it-now you-don't scenario, or that Orlando was in a hurry, which he isn't. Both hands are resting squarely on his hips, his feet are planted slightly apart and his chest appears to have expanded, for he's displaying himself much as a narcissistic peacock might do in the presence of a prospective mate.

I ask Orlando to put his penis away and leave. This handsome thirty-something mulatto, a software engineer, looks baffled and hurt by my rejection.

"You came up here to help me fix the laptop. No guests are permitted in these rooms", I remind him.

"I'm not a guest. I won't be staying overnight ... I'm just visiting..."

"Just go. Go home."

The following afternoon, I ask Elisa whether exposure is common practice in Cuba; she assures me that it's not.

"Cubans are gentlemen. They wouldn't, really they wouldn't …what colour did you say Orlando was again?"

Then she extends her left arm and dabs the skin on the back of her wrist with the index finger of her right hand, looking at me inquiringly. This is the customary Cuban way of indicating mulatto or black. Somehow the gesture is regarded as less open to racist interpretation than the spoken word.

I don't tell my friend what colour Orlando is and I'm surprised that she has raised the issue, considering the ebony tones of her own skin. I'm annoyed that, in her insistence on how well-behaved Cuban men are, she doesn't mention the phenomenon of cinemas and masturbation to me. This is a discovery I'm just beginning to make for myself.

I'm discovering how sexually charged this society is. It's difficult to work out why this might be. Perhaps Cubans have super-powered hormones, but I doubt it. Maybe it's the exotic mix that has produced such spectacularly attractive men and women, constant temptation on a "conveyor belt of human beauty," as Graham Greene wrote in *Our Man in Havana*. There are whites, clear-skinned mulattos, dark-skinned mulattos, black Cubans and also Chinese on the island. Many are a stunning combination, a product of the mix of all these ethnic backgrounds; so it is not uncommon to see European green or blue eyes with honey-coloured or Caribbean coffee complexions. Beautiful women are routinely – and shamelessly – ogled as soon as they set foot in the street Indeed, men appear to have their radar permanently switched on when they are out of doors; whether they're out driving, playing a game of dominos or talking to their wives, they'll pick up the signal and lock on to it, head turning a full 180º to absorb each movement and every detail.

Although it's not unknown for obscene remarks to be made to a passing woman, I have never heard any. It's more often the case that if there's an opportunity, he'll pay her a compliment, a *piropo*, and this is something of an art in Cuba, the art of flattery.

"Hey there gorgeous! You with so many curves and me with no brakes."

To be fair, it's not all one-sided at all. Walking along Obispo Street in Central Havana I see young and not-so-young *cubanas*, women who are eminently comfortable with their bodies, sashaying down the street, wearing the tightest of jeans and skimpiest of tops in a celebration of their shapeliness, a vision that would *make a dead man rise* as Bob Dylan wrote. Flattery, especially if it's original, will be received with a congenial smile and a turn of the head:

"*Muchas gracias.*"

Caribbean women reign supreme in the realm of curves, swaying hips, provocative dress and seductive smile. Sensuality suffuses every cell of their being. As a Celt, I can only hope that my *otherliness* will compensate for the lack of all those charms that my rivals abound in; if not my nights are destined to be lonely ones in Havana. I needn't have worried. Being young (ish), attractive and, above all, foreign is a combination that many Cuban men find tempting, particularly so given that I'm not married and could therefore, potentially become their passport out of poverty.

So, naturally I'm sceptical when Cuban men approach me in the street for a chat. It would be naive not to recognise that there could be an element, maybe even a strong element, of ulterior motives behind any attachment that a Cuban forms with a foreigner. This is evidently the case when there is a significant age difference involved. A fifty-something Norwegian married to a seventeen-year-old from the mountains in the east would be a case in extreme; but it happens because she wants a passport and he wants a young bride.

By the time I meet Jesús, an ENT specialist, and decide to take the initiative, I'm confident of my familiarity with the potential dangers. We meet early one Saturday afternoon, in the Calixto García general hospital, just outside the ENT pavilion, where I've been directed to have an ear condition treated. Jesús is on call, doing 24-hour weekend duty. When I first see him he's sitting alone on a bench, legs outstretched, one hand in the pocket of his white coat, the other, languidly fanning himself with a copy of *Granma* newspaper. I step on to the porch and he looks up with interest, or perhaps it's relief that a patient has come along to deliver him from an otherwise empty and tedious day. It's hot, so he invites me to accompany him inside. Jesús is attractive and well educated. After inquiring about where I'm from he tells me that he is Chilean, his mother is a widow and a refugee from the dictator General Pinochet. I want to impress, so we talk about a few of the well-known heroes dating back to that era in Chile, President Salvador Allende,[i] the poet Pablo Neruda[ii] and singer-songwriter Victor Jara[iii] and then I ask how he feels about his life in Cuba.

Jesús gives serous consideration to this question and the light-hearted mood quickly fades. He's well aware of general frustration with the situation in the country but doesn't share it. His family is deeply indebted to the Revolution and fully supports it, even though there are aspects of day-to-day life in the country that are far from ideal. Jesús and his mother have good reason to support it, they fled military rule in the 1970s and were accepted as refugees on the island shortly afterwards. They had nowhere else to go. He graduated from medical school on a full scholarship two years previously and was accepted at the Calixto García hospital to train to become an ENT specialist, an *otorrinolaringólogo*. There and then I vow to practice all nine syllables of the word at home until I achieve perfection as I'm already hoping I'll be meeting him again, but not for medical treatment.

We've been talking for about half an hour when we hear a knock on the door. Jesús rolls his eyes, gestures to me to be quiet, and we sit in silence. The knocking continues, more insistently this time. I feel uncomfortable, anxious that whoever it is may open the door and catch us sitting here in guilty silence. Thankfully, the shutters on the window are closed and nobody can see us. After thirty seconds or so, during which time I'm sure the interloper has an ear pressed up against the door, we hear footsteps recede along the corridor. Jesús lets out an audible sigh and whispers that he'd better attend to me.

Five minutes later I have a tube running out of my nose into a rubber ball which Jesús squeezes intermittently while I say "Ka Ka Ka." Suddenly the colonial style shutters on the window swing abruptly inward and two nurses peer in at us. They don't hide their irritation,

"So there you are. Doctor Jesús, you know you have patients here waiting to see you."

A queue of about half a dozen faces turn in our direction and peer in at us.

Three days later I see Jesús again. This time we are in the main ENT department, behind the pavilion where I found Jesús the previous Saturday. There are sixty or seventy patients around me sitting on wooden benches in the waiting area. Overhead, the fans have clicked to a halt; the air is thick and heavy with the smell of sweat and stale tobacco. There's a power cut and emergency generators are used only ... for emergencies, for the operating theatre and refrigerating blood supplies. Some patients wander outside but it's too hot and so they linger in the doorway in the hope of catching a breeze. Unsure of what the procedure is, I walk in and join a queue at the front of the room leading up to a hatch type window, built at waist level. Patients stoop to address the ill-tempered nurse in a sharp white uniform perched on a stool on the other side. When it's my turn I see she's beginning to slide the window over, closing the hatch in effect, so I jam my hand into the remaining space and present her with my appointment card.

"We're finished for today."

I stoop further to achieve eye contact.

"I have an appointment with Dr. Mendes."

My accent catches her attention and she barks back that foreigners are not seen in this hospital. I'm a foreign technician, I tell her, working at *Granma*. The look she gives me says she's going to accept this explanation, although with a sulky reluctance. This is a lady who is not accustomed to being contradicted but even she knows better than to challenge the authority of *Granma International*. I'm motioned through into the second waiting area behind her, where a reduced number of patients stand around in clusters, queuing apparently. An hour and a half later I'm ushered through into the third and final area, the treatment room. This is where Jesús repeats the treatment with the rubber ball and tube, and tells me to return the following week. He is much more guarded this time and I wonder whether I imagined his initial enthusiasm in what I have allowed myself to regard as the start of a "getting-to-know-you phase."

On my way out I make a detour into the toilet but halt on the threshold because the stench is sickening. There's a sea of urine covering most of the floor. Little rainbow patterns have formed on the surface, giving it an oil-like sheen. It could have been flooded for hours or even days. I tiptoe across to the cubicles. The first three are overflowing and faeces are bobbing up and down in the bowls. I don't look into the remaining three. My bladder is, I hope, stronger than my stomach, so I withdraw.

After that day I cycle up to the Calixto García hospital whenever Jesús is on 24 hour duty. We sit on the bench outside the pavilion where I first saw him and talk until midnight and then he walks me to the bicycle park and kisses me chastely on the cheek. Sometimes he laughs and occasionally makes me smile. More often though, Jesús is self absorbed and lost in his dark mutterings about the state of his neurones. His depression is not enough to put me off. My interest in him is obvious and yet we don't make progress. Twice he agrees to meet me at my apartment and twice he fails to arrive. I've been stood up, and so "*embarcada*" becomes my latest new word in Cuban Spanish. Elisa laughs off my despair and humiliation.

"It's an offensive ... you're going to win him over. You've just lost two battles, that's all. Don't give up."

Then she adds: "It's easy to see he's not a full-blooded *cubano*. No self-respecting *cubano* would turn down a chance to see you in your apartment."

Her attitude is to embrace the challenge and overcome the difficulties with skill and strategy. Mine is resignation and defeat. Mentally, I've already walked away, cycled away rather, convinced that Jesús is wasting my time when I visit him yet again at the Calixto. Then he phones me at *Granma* to apologise. This is the first time he's ever called so I'm thrilled and agree to meet him that weekend at the Calixto. This time it's me that cancels. On the night when I am due to see Jesús I'm strolling along the sea front with Handsome Amilcar, who is making a surprise visit to me from El Salvador. He's staying for ten days and I want to give him my full attention, but I can't. My main worry is that Jesús will discover I have a male visitor, an attractive one, which makes it difficult to enjoy Amilcar's courtship. Ironically, now that I've stood him up, Jesús is more attentive than ever, phoning me at work every day. He pressures me into inviting him to my apartment on Friday morning. When I've put the phone down I wonder how I'm going to pull it off. Mr. El Salvador is not due to head back home for another five days and I'm supposed to be working....

Elisa is enthusiastic.

"Of course you can do it. Didn't I say that we women win the war with skill, strategy and stealth?"

"You didn't mention stealth before."

"Didn't I? Well, I should have. It's the most important weapon of all."

She offers to take Amilcar to the beach while I'm at work and he agrees, although he'd rather have gone with me.

"Next time, I promise."

He pulls a face and looks momentarily sullen.

"Next time, then."

Once he has disappeared out into the heat of Avenida 20 de mayo, I hastily collect all evidence of his presence – tee shirts, shorts, jeans, socks and rucksack - and shove it into a wardrobe in the spare bedroom. Certain that there is no trace of a man in my apartment, I take the next step: I go into work. After half an hour at my computer I vanish into the toilet, remove my make up, dab some water on my face, wait for a few minutes, and present myself to Liz. I've got the runs, I tell her, and I need to be in my own home. No questions are asked and by ten o'clock I'm looking at my reflection in my bathroom mirror, adding the final touches to my newly made-up eyes. Jesús arrives right on time and, after a courtesy coffee, we make it into bed, at last. Ten minutes later, when we've finished, I finally understand why he procrastinated and cancelled repeatedly, because he has nothing to offer me. Jesús knows nothing of affection, intimacy, warmth, technique or passion. I was blind to this before. Still, there's a relief to know that I can stop pursuing him. I look across at him. Jesús is already history. He'll leave my bed in a moment, walk out of my apartment and be out of my life in less than half an hour and I'm impatient for this to happen.

With no pillow talk to detain us, we both leave the bed at the same time. Just then, as Jesús stands up, the condom slides off his penis and falls to the floor. We both bend to pick it up and in that moment I see two things which deeply unnerve me. First, I notice Amilcar's lace-up brown leather shoes placed neatly under my bed. They are the only items under the bed. A pair of men's sturdy shoes. Moving swiftly, I seize the condom before Jesús can fully stoop to reach it, which is when I notice that he was wearing two, not one. The word *neurótico* slips into my mind but I say nothing because I'm so grateful that he didn't notice Amilcar's shoes and that he'll be nothing more than an uncomfortable memory by the end of the day.

Elisa is highly amused.

"Sex doesn't appear to be his thing at all. Well, at least he wouldn't have cheated on you."

Which would have made him unique on the island, in her view.

All the women I know have had at least one unfaithful partner or, as Cubans put it, they have had "horns put on them." *Pegar los tarros* is one of the first Cuban Spanish phrases that I am taught on my arrival in Havana, and I hear it repeatedly throughout my stay. Is it just men who have this reputation? I'm told that it is both, although the men either have more time to be unfaithful or they're caught out more often by their craftier wives or girlfriends. A man from my neighbourhood was almost burned alive after his wife discovered he was having an affair and didn't hesitate to set fire to him.

"Lots of women have doused their husbands with kerosene and put a match to them," says Elisa.

"I would have done the same too when I was with the girls' fathers, except that I was the mistress. So it was clear from the start there would be another woman in the relationship ... the wife."

A few days later I 'm standing on Calzada del Cerro hoping to hail a Panataxi to take me to the airport to collect some friends visiting from Ireland. One pulls over and a shapely young mulatta gets out of the passenger seat after leaning over to give the driver a kiss full on the lips. She mouths another kiss at him as I'm getting in and tells him she'll see him that evening. As the journey takes about thirty minutes we chat light-heartedly to pass the time, then his mobile rings, interrupting the conversation. It's clear he's talking to his wife, who is phoning from Spain to tell him how much she misses him. I listen to him reassure her that he loves her deeply and that he's counting the days until they are together again.

"Be brave, darling. I'm lonely too but I can hold on. It's not long now. Not tonight, I'm working. Tomorrow, we'll talk again tomorrow. Ciao, ciao, ciao. A big kiss. Mwah."

When he's finished he looks across at me with the expression of a child who has been caught out telling a fib.

I try to be non-judgmental but I can only think of one thing to say and it comes out bluntly, very unsubtly.

"Why?"

"She's been gone five months now and I'm a man with needs and desires. I can't be on my own. It's only natural. Anyway, life's too short."

His story is not unusual. They have a plan, a long-term plan to relocate their entire family in Spain. Phase One began four years previously when they decided to target a Spanish tourist and convince him that he had found the love of his life in the taxi driver's wife.

He smiles at me conspiratorially.

"My wife is a red hot mulatta and nobody can teach her anything about the art of seduction. The Gallego drooled and ogled her night and day. He came back to Cuba six times in the course of a year to be with her. As soon as he proposed marriage we got an express divorce. She hates Spain without me but her citizenship is coming through any day now. When that happens she divorces the Gallego, comes to Cuba and remarries me. We'll be husband and wife again, but not in Havana, in Madrid."

"What are you going to do in Madrid?"

"Start again. It has to be better than here."

I say nothing. The three s's come to mind, stealth, skill and strategy.

When the opportunity arises I ask my women friends about their experiences of infidelity and betrayal.

Marta has been married to Marcelo for thirty years. He used to be an athlete, a trainer for the Olympic shooting team. Now he runs a small up-market guesthouse in the Vedado area of the city with his wife and brother-in-law. I go to their home once or twice a week to use the Internet. They are part of a tiny minority of Cubans who are connected and, like others in that tiny minority, they've made a small business out of it. Friends and neighbours who they trust are allowed to access the Internet from Marcelo's office in return for a modest fee.

Early one evening I've just sent my latest batch of emails and I'm sitting with Marta on the terrace drinking a papaya milkshake. Nobody else is in the house: all the tourists lodging here have gone out, so I raise the subject. She's surprisingly honest and open in her response. Marcelo, she reveals, has been serially unfaithful throughout the course of their marriage. He's had a number of mistresses which Marta found out about again and again. I'm puzzled and intrigued.

"So, why did you stay with him?"

"Because I love him."

Marcelo is the only man she has ever loved and her dream has always been to grow old and die with him. Creating a scandal and kicking him out to live with his mistress would have put paid to that dream. So, each time she found out he was cheating she screamed, cried and raged ... into the pillow or round at the sister's house. At home she redoubled her efforts to retain her husband.

"I dyed my hair, manicured my nails, wore my sexiest clothes, became a better cook and ... a better lover. I became a whore in bed. And, I agreed with a few male friends that they would ring me at the most "inopportune" times. I know my husband's weak points and that's how I kept him. Cunning and tenacity."

Then she looks at her nails and smirks.

"The mistresses lost him because they had no strategy, I did, and I've won. He's mine now and he'll stay by my side until the end because he's too old and too fat to find another mistress for himself."

It's hard to say whether Marta or old age has vanquished Marcelo. Either way it's unlikely that, at age 62, he'll be putting the horns on any woman ever again. But who knows? Viagra isn't available in Cuba...yet.

Mariana is a member of the executive of the Federation of Cuban Women (FMC). She thinks that Marta sacrificed her integrity and self respect in her pursuit of Marcelo.

"Did she tell you how humiliated and disgraced she felt each time she discovered another lover? Did she tell you how defiled she felt when her marriage turned into a web of lies and deception? I know, because it happened to me."

Mariana explains how her husband used to come home late at night, often smelling of another woman, showing little interest in her, beyond criticism of her dress and her nails. Unlike Marta, Mariana confronted her partner and put an end to the marriage. Now she's alone, living in her half of the home she used to share with her husband. A breeze-block wall running through the centre of the house was the only practical solution they could find in a society where housing and money are a scarcity. The wall was built when her husband decided he wanted to live with his mistress. Sounds easily filter through the fragile partition.

"It's some consolation that I hear them fighting about the same things we used to fight about. And he is as critical of her as he used to be with me."

Mariana is the first person to warn me about the unpleasant side of cinema- going in Cuba, although by then, I've already had one or two vivid experiences of my own. She's passionate about cinema and goes regularly, sometimes alone, even though she's aware that the risk of falling victim to the plague of masturbation is much increased when women are unaccompanied by a male partner. We decide to close ranks and buy tickets for the film festival.

Every year Havana hosts the Latin American Film Festival in December. For the ten days that the festival lasts, life in the city seems to revolve around cinema. *Habaneros* make a feast out of the event, as opportunities to see quality films are otherwise generally scarce in Cuba. It is common for many *aficionados* to take two weeks off work and spend ten consecutive days rushing from one screen to the next, cramming in three, or even four films daily. Ironically, outside of the festival, American action productions tend to feature most in the listings, but not always. During my stay in Havana, I get to see a number of European and independent films in the cinemas, for an entrance fee of only 2 pesos, about 3p. This is the standard charge for tickets, so I make the most of it.

On the first afternoon of the festival, the *Rampa* is screening François Truffaut's *The 400 Blows*, which neither Mariana nor I have seen before. We are surprised to discover that the cinema is packed to capacity, of maybe a thousand people, proving that I should never underestimate the Cuban appetite for high-brow European productions.

We take our seats, the lights dim, silence descends and the film begins. I'm uneasy and unable to focus on the performance. My guard is up because a man has just slid into the seat beside me, to my right. There are a couple of unoccupied seats but he has chosen this one. It's a bad sign. Sure enough, within minutes he is masturbating, or at least I think he is. I wait until I'm absolutely certain, and when I am, I swing back my right arm and slap him hard across the back of the head. He groans, hastily fastens his fly and rushes out. There is a murmuring and a commotion in the darkness around me. A woman asks pointedly what he did to deserve such a wallop and I tell her to use her imagination. Mariana, who has noticed nothing, looks at me disconcerted, wondering perhaps about my sanity. I tell her I'll talk to her later about it because I don't want the incident to ruin her night too. Just then a security guard leans over and whispers into my ear, inviting me to accompany him to the manager's office. I get up reluctantly. I'm going to miss the first few minutes of the film but the "invitation" means I have no choice but to cooperate.

The manager introduces himself, shakes my hand, and invites me to step into the office, where there is a man sitting against the wall being interrogated by two police officers.

"Is this yours?"

Yours?

"No, he's not *mine*. *Mine* was wearing a pale blue shirt."

"So, where is he then?"

"He ran out in a hurry after I slapped him."

Both policemen turn to look at me simultaneously. They've heard something now that interests them. I cradle my right hand and rub my thumb across the palm, which is still smarting. There's nothing to be done because *mine* has escaped, so the manager offers to accompany me back to my seat. We walk the empty brown corridor and he apologises on behalf of the cinema for the incident.

"It happens all the time. That's why we have the police here. We know the faces of re-offenders and we blacklist them. They're not allowed back into the cinema. But new ones come. It's a plague. They choose pretty young women and you are very pretty. Have you got a boyfriend?"

I'm used to this. It's par for the course so I smile and mention that my hand is still hurting. Armando, this is his name, tells me to ask for him personally if I should have any further problems at the cinema, and then he departs, with a lingering look in my direction.

A number of advertisements, or public warnings, have been broadcast on television highlighting the problem. Masturbation in cinemas, it seems, has reached epidemic proportions. It certainly has for me. I've fallen victim so many times that I have adopted a strategy: I enter the cinema and take a seat next to a woman or women, or a couple, away from unaccompanied males, but still I'm targeted. During *American Beauty* I am obliged to change seat three times. On the first occasion I'm sitting next to a couple, yet, as soon as the lights dim, the empty seat to my right is occupied. He must have chosen the moment to slide in under cover of darkness; within five minutes I'm up on my feet in a fluster and looking for another seat. Twice more the same routine is repeated and I'm in a rage because, yet again, my trip to the movies has turned into another sordid experience, but I refuse to surrender. Instead, I relocate for a fourth time and, sunk deep into my seat, listen resignedly as the rhythmic creaking behind me gathers momentum. Then it's silent again and gingerly I touch the top of my head. It's conceivable... but my hair is dry.

On screen, Annette Bening is screaming at Kevin Spacey: "Do you think you're the only one who's frustrated?"

CHAPTER 4

On The Road

Gently does it, gently, g-e-n-t-l-y. Perfect. That's just the way I like it.

Then with a satisfied smile he reaches for the volume and I'm blasted with salsa. No surprise that he loves *Los Van Van*, the kings of double entendre in Cuba.

He's my driver and he's only talking about closing the car door, of course. But even such a mundane request is an opportunity for any red-blooded *cubano* to flirt, and to flirt with style. I slide into my seat and he flashes me a sidelong look as he shifts gear, I grin to let him know that his innuendo is appreciated. I'm in a *máquina*, a collective taxi, along with five other passengers and we've just left Central Havana en route to La Lisa, one of the more downbeat neighbourhoods in the city.

It's stifling and every window in the vehicle is wound down. In fact, the windows are permanently wound down. They've probably been wound down since they broke some time back in the 1950s. It's sad that in the half century or so since this car began its journey, not everybody has treated it gently. It's battered and bent but it has spirit and it's still on the road. We are purring along in a black Chevrolet that hiccups every now and again when we hit a pothole, or burps unceremoniously when the clutch is called into action. But who cares if this old lady shows her age from time to time? This is the Zsa Zsa Gabor of the road and I know I'm blessed to be one of the last few to luxuriate in her charms before she retires.

I've been living in Havana for almost a year now and I'm still bewitched by these elegant pre-revolution era cars. Each time I hail one I am glee-filled and have to suppress the desire to jump up and down on the spot that I can, with a mere wave of the hand, halt one of these beauties and avail of her charms. I frequently stop and gawk at them, giving myself away as a foreigner in the process. But I can't disguise my feelings. It's their aura; they unfailingly exude sophistication and timelessness. They are forever associated with a bygone era of Hollywood film stars and real-life mafia, a golden era when they were young, happy, and forever beautiful.

Roads populated with these vintage cars fuel my daydreams and fantasies. On Calzada del Cerro a 1938 Packard pulls to a halt unexpectedly in front of me. I stare. It's a sinister manoeuvre and I expect to see half a dozen raincoated gangsters hastily emerge wielding violin cases. Instead, two women wearing fluorescent pink and lime green lycra leggings step out into the hot sunshine. *Ciao, Ciao*, they smile happily and their friend waves back to them from the rear window. The Packard drifts away and for a few moments it is the only vehicle on the road. I see it doggedly zigzagging past potholes, framed against a background of crumbling façades of 19th century architecture. Then it is gone, and I'm left alone with my fantasy.

This is a route I take when visiting friends in La Lisa. When I'm in a hurry I take a *máquina*, it's comfortable but self-indulgent because, at 10 pesos, it often feels like an unnecessary extravagance. The *máquina* is twenty five times the cost of a bus ride or fifty times the price of a *camello* ticket.

If the Chevrolet is Zsa Zsa Gabor then the *camello*, a camel bus, is the Medusa of the road. They are something of a monster designed to transport around 250 people, or more. *Camellos,* officially called Metro buses, first appeared in Cuba in the early nineties, at the start of the Special Period, when fuel shortages were critical and spare parts almost non-existent. At the time they were a practical and necessary response to the need to move tens of thousands of commuters around the capital as economically as possible. People could only get so far on their Chinese bicycles.

You hear the *camello* before you catch sight of it. You can often smell it too. *Camellos* belch thick black diesel fumes from an exhaust pipe in the roof, to the accompaniment of much rumbling and wheezing.

"I guess they're not big on smog control here," an American tourist said to me one morning, coughing violently, when we were caught behind a *camello* on our bicycle tour of Havana.

Boarding one of these monsters is an act of bravery, foolishness, or both. But it's a challenge I can't resist, particularly when I am tempted to test myself, to see if I can withstand the hardships that Cubans face daily, day in, day out. It's like dipping my toe into deep and dangerous waters, momentarily deluding myself that I can swim these currents just like everybody else. But I doubt whether I have the stamina. It's a fantasy, just like the Packard. The *camello* could break me.

Tonight I've just left my good friend Beatriz's home. I don't feel like indulging in the luxury of a ten peso *máquina* ride so I pause at the nearby bus stop on Calzada de Cerro. My heart sinks when I see that there are already about forty people hovering around. My nerve weakens when nobody responds to my call for the last person in the "queue." I feel foolish but I continue walking meekly from cluster to cluster until I finally locate the man in front of me. He's wearing blue jeans and a red baseball shirt. When the throng moves forward I have to fall into line behind this man, behind these colours. Suddenly, he's hailed a *máquina* and vanished into its interior. There's a void left behind in the queue. This has happened to me before and I should have learned the lesson. It's not enough to locate the last person, the one before him has to be identified too, as a contingency. It's *de rigueur* and I forgot. Now I'm stranded. I'll be mortified if the next person to join the queue asks who is in front of me. Replying "dunno" is embarrassing, especially if you have taken pride — as I have — in being as adroit as any *habanero* on this battlefront.

Just then I hear the *camello* approach. It is climbing the hill and will soon appear around the bend. The throng stiffens to attention and musters closer to the stop. A couple of passers-by step hastily out of the way and into the road, taking a detour rather than get caught up in the impending scrum; it's not unknown for "innocents" to be sucked into a *camello* by the sheer force of pushing and shoving. I feel the adrenaline surge, look for a vantage point, and silently vow to take a *máquina* next time. Checking that my purse is wedged into the bottom of my bag and that the zip is fully closed, I step forward. The camel shudders to a halt, the doors open and the passengers don't exactly alight: they are spewed forth into the night. Meanwhile the tight scrum has divided, like a swarm of angry bees, into two, each mustering around a different entrance and launching the offensive even before the last passenger, a woman, has emerged. She sees the deluge and looks frightened, fearful that she may not make it down the steps onto the street, but she does, although almost without her skirt. She grabs the folds, which had been momentarily swept back into the *camello* with the rush, and tugs hard, hastily rearranging the flowing garment around her before stomping off.

I choose the rear entrance. There's a tiny gap that I know I can slide into. And I do. With my bag tucked securely under my right arm I deftly manoeuvre myself up the steps and weave my way into the heart of the densely packed vehicle. I've learned not to stand close to the exit because this is where most movement occurs as passengers enter and exit. Tussles can become fraught and it's not uncommon for heated exchanges to take place if someone fears they are going to miss their stop. A further reason to avoid the exit is pickpockets. A hand can slip into a pocket or a bag in the very instant the *camello* pulls to a halt. Two seconds later the perpetrator is gone, out into the street, and the wall of people closes over again. There's nothing you can do about it.

Tonight I'm hanging from a safety strap, close to a window which is jammed open, so I have reason to feel pleased. It's something of a coup, because the ride to La Lisa takes about forty minutes. There's no air conditioning on the *camello*, or indeed on any form of public transport in Cuba, except for the hard-currency Panataxis. The temperature outside is around 30º with 85% humidity and from in here those figures sound refreshing. We're in a mobile sauna. Sweat drips from the brows of men and dark stains form around the armpits of neatly pressed shirts. Women (with room to) flick their fans desperately but it's of no avail, beads of sweat ooze relentlessly from the pores just above their lips. I stare at the droplets, fascinated, and wonder if my glands are working overtime too. I'm pressed in on all sides, I can't reach for my handkerchief so I lick, and lick again, stretching my tongue as high as possible to catch the drops before they trickle down onto the woman seated directly beneath where I'm standing.

Nobody knows for certain how many people fit into a *camello*. Nobody has ever gauged its capacity. There'd be no fun in testing it. Tonight is average; a bony shoulder is wedged into my back and there is friction between my hips and those of the woman dangling from the strap to my right. As we pull in to stop, the engine groans and metal screeches. There is frantic movement behind me. I grip tighter. Passengers lurch toward the exit and, hissing, we jerk to a halt. The *camello* lets out a long slow sigh as a score or so board in a frenzy. A new contingent jostles behind me. One is a cigar smoker. His mouth must be less than five centimetres from the back of my neck. I'm just beginning to worry that my hair will smell of stale Cohiba when I feel another development take place. I want to believe that it's a bony hip jamming into my ass, but I know it's not. This is a familiar experience and I weigh up my options. A slapped face is not one of them. I can barely move my head, much less turn around to get a swing at him. I can't shuffle forward as I'm already jammed against the window. Sideways I'm blocked too. I freeze, staring fixedly ahead and hope that he'll go away. He doesn't, of course. Slowly and deliberately I prise my right foot out from its docking place and raise it. Glancing down slyly at the culprit's feet I slam down hard. The effect is immediate. With a sharp intake of breath and a curse he withdraws into the ranks behind him. No one takes his place.

With their typical wit Cubans call the *camello* the Saturday night movie, the X-rated movie, with guaranteed sexual content, bad language and violence. On the M4 route to La Lisa, it's easy to see why. Groping, curses and pick-pocketing are par for the course and nobody is surprised when the journey is peppered with this kind of unpleasantness. In reality, this is only one part of the drama. Kindness and courtesy too, as well as humour, are nearly always apparent. In the midst of the pushing and shoving, seats are quickly yielded to the elderly, to pregnant women, and there's always room for some light-hearted flirting, so often the case in Cuba.

At the heart of it all is the conductor, the man who weaves and pirouettes his way through the knot of passengers collecting payment for the fare. These are the real heroes of the *camello*. The conductor often has an enduring sense of humour, crucial when he is called in to mediate between angry passengers, as well as a keen eye for the ladies. Our conductor tonight is no exception. He is smiling impishly at the attractive forty-something who has just boarded by the middle entrance, right behind me. He glides down the central aisle to take her fare and I notice that his hand lingers just a couple of seconds longer than is necessary over hers as he places the change in her palm.

"*Muchas gracias, señora.*"

She glances up at him coyly: "*Señorita*, you mean."

The crowd murmurs its approval at the speed of her rejoinder, and she tosses her head high, flicks her hair and threads her way toward the back of the bus with a satisfied smile. A couple of male passengers follow her with their gaze. This lady oozes confidence and style, and they like it.

Not all men express their interest by jamming their erection into me in the *camello*. One evening I'm squeezing sideways through the throng of passengers, attempting to bundle myself out of the exit before the *camello* moves on from my stop. A slightly-built mulatto in a medic's white coat turns and whispers that he's getting off too.

"Stay right behind me. I've done this a thousand times."

We descend and the doors slam shut right behind me. The man in the white coat politely withdraws the hand he extended to support me when I step out on to the kerb.

"You're a doctor, then?"

"And you're a foreigner, then?"

I've just met Alexis, the man who makes me forget all my own rules about avoiding relationships with Cuban men. It is early evening and we stroll along Avenida 51 chatting amiably, flirting mildly, unaware that his wife, a blonde woman, was following at a distance.

"I'm divorced," he smiles. "What about you?"

Alexis tells me he is an anaesthetist.

"Not a real doctor, you see. I rarely have much to do with patients. I just put them to sleep and when I do, all that matters to me is their vital signs. Real doctors get to know their patients but I'm more of a scientist than a doctor. Chemistry is my first love but my parents sent me to medical school because they thought it would be useful to have a medic in the family."

"Is it?"

"Well, yes. I can easily deal with family emergencies, but what's even more useful are the contacts I have among specialists at the hospital where I work. So if there is a real emergency I phone my colleagues and get an appointment with them."

Alexis explains that he was in Vedado looking for a house for his parents. They want a *permuta*. They're trying to swap their large dilapidated home in the Siboney area for something more modest and in better condition.

"In reality, they don't want to move house. Their place in Siboney is a beautiful early 20th century mansion which belonged to the Bacardí family before they fled Cuba in 1959. But it's falling to pieces now because my parents have never been able to afford the repair work. You should see it – there's a stained glass dome presiding over the entrance in the hall and the entire house is built around a garden, cloister style, where banana and avocado trees grow. Money is a problem and so they're hoping to make about ten thousand dollars from the swap."

Buying or selling a home is illegal in Cuba. The state alone has the right to deal in property so the only way to change residence is to swap ... if you have something to swap. Money is not permitted to change hands but in practice it nearly always does, particularly if one of the parties is acquiring a larger home than the one he or she is swapping. In this case a sum of money – always cash – would accompany the deal.

Alexis explains that his parents have contracted a broker, someone with knowledge of who wants to swap in Havana, and what it is they are looking for. When an agreement is reached the broker takes commission from both parties.

"It's a tidy living for some. So far though, we haven't had much luck. This is the second year of searching and nothing has come of it. People just don't have the money that my parents need."

Alexis asks how long I have been living in Havana and what I'm doing here. He looks startled when I say that I'm working for *Granma International* but I laugh and reassure him that I'm not state security.

"But *I* could be. Be very careful of what you say. You never know who you are talking to in this country."

I tell him that I'm leaving my job the following week and that I would have left before had I discovered a way to remain in the country without the work visa from *Granma*. The minute I leave the job, the welcome mat with a residence permit will be withdrawn.

"Now I can finally leave. The Cuban authorities have just approved the application my newspaper editor submitted to them back in April. I'll be able to stay here legally as a foreign correspondent, a freelance journalist. Cuba is not a strict priority for my editor, so it means I'll have to supplement my income by working on freelance translations and in tourism, as a tour leader for an American company with a license to operate in Cuba."

As I turn to leave him, Alexis tells me that he'd like to meet me again ... and I'd like to meet him too. He's the first Cuban man I've met whose approach could be described as discreet and I invite him to call me in a couple of week's time. First I have to move house and then I'm going on tour with a group of American teachers.

Then I ask about his ethnic mix. His looks are an exotic combination of oriental eyes, a broad African nose and honey-coloured skin. He's very slight too, probably only a couple of kilos heavier than me, at most.

"I'm Chinese, African and partly Spanish too. Both sets of great grandparents came from China and married mulattos in Cienfuegos, people whose forebears had been slaves on the sugar cane plantations there. My son is blonde. He takes after my ex wife, who is whiter than you are. Our whole family is a melting pot in itself."

Alexis gives me a polite kiss on the cheek and walks away folding the scrap of paper I've given him with my new future telephone number scribbled on it.

"Just give me your number. No need for your name. Do you think I could forget it?"

That evening I begin the process of packing. In three days I will be leaving Avenida 20 de mayo and moving in with Liliana, who lives in Calle San Francisco, a quiet street in an older part of Cerro, about a twenty-minute walk from my apartment. Liliana's home is a ground floor apartment in a three-storey building dating back to the 1930s. The living room is sparsely furnished, although the two sets of shelves on the wall above the dining table are burdened with an array of tacky ornaments, the like of which would only be seen in junk shops back home. The sofa and armchair are made of olive-green plastic, making them sticky and unpleasant to sit on. My bedroom is the largest of the two and is reached via a long hallway leading off the living room. We have agreed a monthly rent of $100, including bills.

Liliana is a lively heavy-set woman in her early sixties. Tall, with curly grey-blonde hair, blue eyes and white skin, she looks like she's from a different continent to most of the others on her street and, indeed, in her neighbourhood. She hates the sun and hasn't been to the beach since she was a teenager. Neither has she been abroad.

"You," she tells me, "are the closest I have ever been to foreign travel. I would love to leave Cuba, but I've nowhere to go. Without money or a family to welcome me I'm stranded here on this island."

Liliana welcomes me into her home on that first Saturday morning with freshly-brewed coffee and a small plate of *cocitos* which are even tastier than Elisa's. Having company around after so many months of living alone may take some getting used to but I'm convinced it will be good for me. I felt vulnerable and lonely for much of the time I lived in the apartment and now I have someone to talk to. And Liliana loves to chat. She sits on my bed while I unpack and talks about her life, or comments on my clothes as I remove them from the suitcase. Everything is *bello*, just beautiful, and her eyes light up again and again. Having her in my room as an audience makes me uncomfortably aware of how affluent I am in comparison, so I cut out the display and hastily bundling the garments into the wardrobe, cutting out the display.

Liliana never married again after her husband was killed in action in Angola,[iv] and they had no children. In recent years she has supplemented her widow's pension by taking in laundry and caring for an elderly neighbour whose family in Miami sends him remittances every few months, out of which he pays Liliana.

On that first weekend I don't learn much more about my landlady because I have to leave Havana on the Monday to begin work on a ten-day tour of the island with a group of US teachers. As I walk out of the door, I'm already looking forward to my return. Liliana has been kind in a grandmotherly fashion and besides, Alexis promised to phone me as soon as I get back

A few days later, I'm travelling with the group when our coach is caught up in the celebrations being held to welcome home Elián González. This little boy has finally returned to Cuba seven months after the court battle began. The US authorities have ruled in favour of his father, Juan

Miguel, who made the journey to Miami to plead for his son to be returned to him in Cuba. Shortly after the ruling, Elián flies into Havana accompanied by his father, baby step-brother and step-mother. International news teams capture the moment. They also flash images of hard-line Miami Cubans who remain sourly silent in the midst of the festivities, possibly recognising that they have shot themselves in the foot by arguing that they were rescuing Elián from a communist dictatorship. Juan Miguel doesn't look like an evil cadre; he is a charming honest-faced hotel worker who just wanted his son back home. As far as he was concerned, Elián had been abducted. "Kidnapped" was the term the Cuban government used, and it stuck on the island.

Elián's return is a massive victory by the authorities. For days the image of him descending the aircraft steps at José Martí international airport is broadcast repeatedly on Cubavision news. Large crowds line the streets in the child's hometown of Cárdenas to welcome the victory parade. The majority are undoubtedly delighted that Elián is back home and that Cuba has won an important battle with the US. However, some of those cheering are quietly relieved that since the saga has finally drawn to a close they will be freed from the obligation to attend the weekly mass mobilisations.

On that afternoon in June 2000 our coach is part of the sprawling traffic jam blocking the usually quiet streets of Cárdenas. All around us drivers sound their horns rhythmically and a sea of people brandish mini Cuban paper flags on sticks, waving them frantically, as they always do at any mass protest or celebration. I see half a dozen middle-aged women, grouped in the shade under one of the few trees on the street, flicking their fans listlessly under their chins. There is no hint of a breeze. Many of those lining the streets are primary school children dressed in their maroon and white uniforms, topped with the blue neckerchief of the pioneers, the children's Communist organisation. The victory parade isn't due for another couple of hours but the crowds are delighting in the anticipation. Our coach could be caught here until sundown, but that is the price we pay for being witnesses to history. The mood all around us is jubilant, so if we are peeved, it would be better to hide it. I look across and see that our driver is finding this difficult. A grim smile is fixed on his face but his red-veined eyes betray his exhaustion. I'm tired too. I scan the scene for an opening which will lead us in the direction of the east-west highway.

Over to my right I catch sight of a horse and carriage amidst the swirl of people and vehicles. The driver is yanking the reins wildly in an endeavour to get the horse to move, but it's not clear in which direction he wants the animal to go, because they are boxed in by the morass. The horse can't fathom it either and it's tossing its head around wildly and lifting its hooves uncertainly. The yanking becomes more impatient and the horse's head is jerked up and down, and left to right. The bit is being used to punish it now and the horse fights back. Half-a-dozen passengers seated in the carriage look on impassively.

With each new jolt the whites of the animal's eyes become wilder and flecks of foam fly from its mouth. Dark patches of sweat shadow its chestnut coat. Finally, the horse attempts to take a couple of hesitant sidesteps, a manoeuvre which is impossible given that it is harnessed to a carriage that is hemmed in, unable to move in any direction. The driver brings the whip down on the bony flank and the horse whinnies and steps hesitantly forward. The whip is brought down again. Just then one of the passengers alights, says something to the driver, and gestures for the whip. He takes the handle, which I notice has been sharpened into a point and buries it into the animal's ribs, sadistically twisting it first one way and then the other to force it deeper into the flesh. The horse is frantic with pain and confusion and rears its head and ululates its despair. All around the flag-waving continues unabated. All heads are turned toward the west, toward the route that Elián's victory cavalcade will take to enter Cárdenas. Just then our bus slides into an opening that the driver has spotted in the crowd and we take a back road to the main highway. I listen to the background chatter of my tour group but there is no hint of discordance. Perhaps I was the solitary witness to this barbarity.

The following day I see a dead horse in Revolution Square in Santa Clara. It is still harnessed to the carriage load of passengers it was pulling when its life ended. The tour group behind me doesn't notice the scene because they are grouped around the gigantic statue of Che Guevara overlooking the plaza, cameras clicking methodically. Our tour guide follows my gaze over to the back of the square. His features darken momentarily and he swears under his breath, muttering something about the time having come to educate people about how to treat animals. We exchange glances; he sighs and turns to answer a question one of the group members has just called out to him. I sit on the steps of the monument watching the passengers get out of the carriage and wander across the heat-seared square burdened with bags and boxes. The driver stands alone with the carcass of his livelihood.

The image of that carcass remains with me for days, and is still on my mind when I return to Havana and walk into Liliana's living room. She looks up and smiles broadly.

"A man phoned three times while you were away. He's keen to talk to you and wanted to know when you'd be home. Alexis, he's called Alexis."

I can't smile back. The image of the dead horse still haunts me.

CHAPTER 5

Santería and the Spirits

Deisy has just gone into a trance. A half-filled glass of water is sitting on the table in front of her and she's staring at it intently. Her fingers are fully outstretched, tips flattened white against her chocolate-brown forehead. After a few moments' silence she jerks her head up and locks her gaze on to me with no hint of recognition; suddenly I'm a stranger to her. She surveys the others gathered around the table through narrowed eyes. There's an energy sharpening her features that wasn't there when she sat down a couple of minutes earlier. Then she begins.

"The spirit tells me ...."

In some countries it's called witchcraft. Here in Cuba it's known as *Santería*, a syncretic religion mixing Catholicism with Yoruba beliefs brought to the island with slaves from West Africa in colonial times. Prohibited from practicing their own religion, the slaves fused it with the Catholicism of their masters. These beliefs, under the guise of Christianity, survived and evolved in the harsh conditions of the sugar and tobacco plantations, and beyond. Today Santería is very probably the most widely practiced religion on the island, among both the white and black population. Evidence of it is everywhere, in the exclusively white garments worn by those being initiated into the faith, in the multi-coloured beads believers wear in honour of their saint or *orisha*, and in the shrines set up in homes across the island.

Deisy is known locally as a *santera*, a holy woman who has special powers that endow her with insights and premonitions which she uses for the benefit of others, for those who call on her help. The version of Santería she practices is perhaps even more syncretic, for it is blended with spiritism; spirits of the dead guide and advise her, offering remedies for personal predicaments and physical ailments. My predicament, she believes, is the consequence of a malign influence in my life; somebody has put a spell on me and Deisy is determined to break that spell.

I'm more intrigued than sceptical so I agree when she urges me to allow her to call on the power of her spirits to help break what I personally believe to be a run of bad luck. A number of ill-fated, potentially disastrous events have overshadowed the last couple of months, making me wonder whether the time has come to pack up and leave for home earlier than I'd planned. First, my bicycle was hit by a motorbike travelling at high speed, although seconds before impact I'd somehow managed to leap to safety. A couple of weeks later, my Russian friend Tatiana's dog attacked me and I nearly lost an eye. Then my laptop overheated and crashed repeatedly, sabotaging my livelihood as a translator in the process. Being superstitious, I feared the omens. I'd escaped without serious injury twice but I might not be so lucky a third time. I certainly wasn't convinced that a spell had been cast, or that the "evil eye" was on me; however, I had been told that Deisy was quite a remarkable *santera* and it was her that I wanted to see, irrespective of whether she could help or not.

Deisy is a heavyset black woman in her early sixties. She is short and round, very round in both body and face. Her neck is concealed under a triple chin that rests upon roll after roll of abundant flesh. With her button-black eyes and ebony hair, she is the gingerbread woman. When she smiles there's a sparkle about her that makes her look content with her life. In reality, Deisy has little to be content about. Two sons have emigrated to the United States and she has seen neither since they left Cuba. One is serving a prison sentence, and the other has worked in a series of unskilled, unstable low-paid jobs that break up the monotony of long spells of unemployment. He sends money from time to time, whenever he can. Deisy's third son, Ricardo, was born late in her life and has significant learning difficulties as well as a physical disability. He's also homosexual, which some of her neighbours regard as his biggest handicap, although they don't say so openly. *Es pájaro*, queer, they whisper, rolling their eyes while flicking their right wrist in an exaggeratedly affected fashion. Those listening often nod sympathetically.

To support herself and Ricardo, Deisy works twelve hour shifts at the local bakery on alternate days. Her earnings are not enough to live on, even though she receives a small pension from the state in recognition of Ricardo's disability. Friends help out whenever they can with small gifts of food and clothes. Liliana gives her lunch from time to time in exchange for a "consultation" with the spirits. I ask Liliana how she manages to embrace two sets of beliefs, beliefs that are highly contradictory: for Liliana is a Jehovah's Witness and regularly attends Bible class.

"I'm a Witness but I'm also Cuban. Santería is where my roots are buried, it's my culture, and it's what I grew up with. Besides, I want to cover my back; it's like an additional insurance, just in case …".

Tatiana has joined the three of us – Deisy, Liliana and me – at the table this evening. She's Russian so these are not her roots, but she adheres to Santería as closely as any Cuban might. She has lived on the island for over thirty years and has adopted the language and the culture as her own. Rarely does Tatiana use her mother tongue now, or even speak of the country she was born in.

"It doesn't even exist any longer, as far as I'm concerned. I wouldn't recognise it now. The USSR has vanished, as have the people I grew up with. There's no reason for me ever to go back there."

So, here we are, all four of us, waiting for Deisy's spirit to tell us whether a spell has been put on me. The others look solemn, they're taking this seriously. I'm mildly embarrassed that I've agreed to participate in this gathering, although the embarrassment fades when Deisy informs us, in a voice that is thick and ponderous, that her spirit is going to take her on a journey in search of the malign influence in my life. Then she pauses briefly, breathes deeply, and begins. She tells us that she is taking a step up from the street and into the porch of my house (an old terraced building in Belfast). She explains how there is a large plant set directly behind the door (which is true) and that there's a chimney to her left as she enters the living room (also true). Now she has my full attention, for her description of the details is startlingly accurate. I have never previously witnessed these kinds of clairvoyant powers so I hear her words in a state of semi-disbelief.

Her journey through my house continues up the stairs to the two bedrooms, one on either side, and on to a room, a strange room "stuck to the roof." It's an attic. She's never seen one and scarcely knows what it is. Then she stops, looks puzzled and asks pointedly,

"Who is Antonio?"

I'd almost forgotten about Antonio, my Spanish boarder from a decade previously. Antonio rented the back bedroom for three years, coming and going without making much impact on me or the household routine. Now, he has unexpectedly surfaced here in my new life in Havana. Hearing his name discomfits me, evoking old concerns about how seriously I may have offended him by increasing the rent or helping myself to his supply of milk.

"Antonio is not the source of your troubles. Envy is the source of your troubles. There is a couple, a Cuban and foreigner, man and woman, you must be wary of."

I ask Deisy to tell me more, but after these revelations her message becomes disappointingly vague. Apparently, I'm shadowed by a restless spirit who sabotages my relationships and clings to me. She urges me to use caution in my choice of friends and men, particularly in my choice of men. She ends by saying that I have to undergo a *rompimiento*, spell-breaking ceremony three days from now in order to be free. Then she shudders, inhales deeply, exhales noisily, and closes her eyes. When she opens them moments later, the energy, that look of being possessed has gone. I don't know what to say.

Liliana is the first to leave the table and she fetches some coffee. Deisy swallows hers in two short gulps and asks me how I feel about what I've heard. I'm astonished, and I tell her so. She smiles.

"But does any of it make sense to you?"

That the details of my house were entirely accurate neither pleases nor displeases her. When I mention my perplexity as to whom this mysterious couple might be, Deisy advises that patience and an open mind will hint at their identity. In the meantime there is the spell-breaking ceremony, for which I have to buy honey, a candle, a cigar, fresh white flowers, basil, cinnamon and a small bottle of rum. Deisy will be back on Tuesday to perform it. As she's leaving she turns to me:

"Oh! Wear old clothes because I have to rip them off you."

After she's gone Liliana quizzes me about my house. She's keen to know about the chimney and what it is like with a roaring fire in it on a cold winter's night.

"But then I've never experienced a cold winter's night, so it's hard for me to imagine how comforting a fire and a hearth might be."

Tatiana is quiet, pensive, saying very little. Finally she confesses to being peeved:

"Deisy has never revealed herself to be that clairvoyant with me when I've asked for help. She has tried but she blocks. I've had to go and talk to a *babalao* in Central Havana." A *babalao* is a priest in the Santería religion.

"He's very good; he can break the power of the evil eye and can tell you who your *orisha* (saint) is. I'll give you his number ... just in case."

On Tuesday morning I'm ready for Deisy. Finding the cinnamon was not the only difficult part of my shopping list. Fortunately, Liliana gave me directions to a local vendor specialising in the sale of "ingredients" favoured by practitioners of Santería. I followed a labyrinthine passageway through a decaying colonial-era building in Cerro until I reached a courtyard, where an ancient mulatto with oriental features and green eyes welcomed me into his tiny apartment with a smile. Flowers, mostly white, but also sunflowers, were arranged on his living room table together with a selection of herbs, honey and multi-coloured beads. The *anciano* puffed heartily on a Cohiba cigar as he handed my bundle across to me. On my way out I greeted a white-robed teenage girl, who seemed bemused to see a foreigner hurrying off embracing a clutch of ingredients for a Santería ceremony.

Deisy arrives slightly earlier than we had arranged and accompanies me to my bedroom to begin the *rompimiento* ritual. We place a basin full of water on the floor in the centre of the room, close to the bed. Motioning me to stand beside it, she lights the candle, takes a swig of rum, and begins to chant words I do not understand under her breath in long heavy tones, while gazing intently at the basin of water. When she has added a few drops of honey to the water, Deisy commands me to step barefoot into the basin. The chanting intensifies, becoming deeper and more urgent, more masculine. Taking rapid puffs of the cigar, she "cleanses" me with the bouquet of flowers and herbs in repeated large downward motions from my head to my knees. With a piece of hard dry bread, Deisy completes the ritual by brushing me vigorously and she continues until the bread disintegrates in her hand, leaving only crumbs floating on the water. Finally, still chanting, she takes a pair of scissors and cuts my clothes off, allowing them to fall into the basin. To end, she takes something that looks like a ball of chalk and draws a circle on the floor around me.

The chanting has ceased now and Deisy leaves the room. I get dressed, open the louvre window slats to their widest and waft the air with a copy of *Granma* newspaper to encourage the departure of the pungent odour of Cohiba. I feel no different, a little nonplussed, perhaps.

When I take Deisy some coffee, she looks pale, worn out. It is very important, she stresses, to bundle the clothes that she cut off me into a bag together with any remaining bread and to get rid of it today, as far away from home as possible.

"Take it to the cemetery, if you can. That's the best place for a malign influence, among the dead, where it can do no harm. I have removed the evil from your life. You are free now."

In the days that follow I reflect repeatedly on this woman's clairvoyance. It enabled Deisy to undertake a psychic journey that took her right into my house in Ireland. She has to be remarkably gifted to do this because there is no way she could have "cheated" since I have no photos of the house with me in Cuba and I have never described the layout to her, or indeed to anyone. Nor have I mentioned or even thought about Antonio since I came to Cuba. If she can do this then perhaps she is right and there is a negative influence or presence in my life. And if that is true, maybe the spell-breaking ceremony can eliminate it. Only time will tell. I'm in awe of her, but I'm also guarded, for I know that today she is on my side but tomorrow that could change. I'm worried about offending her inadvertently.

Cubans have a tendency to be volatile, quick to fly off the handle, and that's when resentment sets in. I pledge to be extra vigilant to ensure that my relations with Deisy don't sour. These are my thoughts when I decide to pay her a visit in her home out of gratitude for her help. I've bought a bunch of flowers, an assortment of toiletries, and I have a donation to make to the *orisha* (saint). Deisy could not have performed the *rompimiento* without the presence and guidance of her *orisha*. According to tradition, the *orisha* mounts or possesses the *santera*, who is then under their control for the duration of the ritual. So, the gifts are, strictly speaking, for the *orisha*.

A long narrow passage leading directly off the busy *Calzada 10 de octubre* takes me to Deisy's home. It is the last in a line of rundown dwellings that were formerly rooms, possibly servants' quarters, in the dilapidated 18th century building where she lives. This building is what is now known as a multi-family dwelling inhabited by a dozen or so families, each of which occupy two or three rooms that have been adapted into independent living areas. The space that Deisy occupies with her son Ricardo, once a single large room, has been divided by a breeze-block partition built at some stage in the past thirty or forty years. We sit in the kitchen while Ricardo lies on the bed on the other side of the partition and watches television. Just behind us, in the corner, is a large statue of Saint Lazarus (known by Santería practitioners as *Babalu Ayé*), which dominates the room. Behind the front door is a coconut shell, painted and decorated with seashells to form the features of the squat figure of *Eleggua*, who is the *orisha* of paths and gateways, which lead either to fortune or misfortune. The preferred place for *Eleggua* is close to the threshold, or close to any of the doors in the home.

We sit on white plastic chairs, the kind we use for picnics or garden furniture back in Ireland, and drink coffee. A pot of black bean stew is simmering in the kitchen, issuing forth clouds of steam laced with a rancid odour that makes me think of overused hospital gowns boiling in a cauldron of stagnant greasy water. When a wave of nausea fills me I know pork is in there amongst the beans. I complain of feeling hot and ask for permission to open the door. Deisy gestures generously toward the latch and I reach for it without rising from my seat. Conditions are so cramped that we are never more than a few steps away from the entrance. Even Saint Lazarus, just to my left, could reach the latch with his crutch, if he was inclined to do so, and he is at the farthest extreme of the room. This is the most abject dwelling I've yet seen. It's impossible to imagine what decade after decade of living in such stunted and squalid conditions does to a person, and yet Deisy has managed to raise three sons in this place. Not for the first time do I feel the immense good fortune of having been born in relatively privileged conditions in Europe. When it is time to leave I present her with my gift and her eyes sparkle as soon as she unwraps the toiletries. For a moment I hope that the perfumed soap and the shampoo will afford her some dignity as she washes herself from a bucket of water that she drains into a hole in the floor of her bathroom.

Deisy has made me much more aware of how prevalent Santería is in so many aspects of life in Cuba. Down on the beach I watch a couple performing a ritual with a dove; on almost every street in Central Havana I see initiates dressed head-to-toe in white, whilst other practitioners wear symbolic coloured beads around their necks and wrists in honour of their *orisha*; in a gutter in Old Havana lie the lifeless remains of a brightly-coloured rooster, and in Colón Cemetery I catch a glimpse of strange tightly-bound packages, resembling miniature corpses, that have been tossed into a grave.

When Deisy introduces me to Roberto, a *babalao* from Central Havana, I ask him about these mysterious packages. He frowns momentarily and then explains that they are probably the work of *paleros*, practitioners of Palo Monte, which is a religion originally from Congo, Zaire and

Mozambique. Some people accuse the *paleros* of engaging in black magic rituals, but he is diplomatic:

"I'm a *babalao* and my religion is Santería so it wouldn't be fair for me to comment on the truth of that."

Roberto is the blackest Cuban I've seen so far, almost blue black, and he's dressed entirely in white, a smart pristine white suit topped by a white cap. He invites me to his home so that he can introduce me to one of the most common Santería rituals, which uses coconut shells. It takes me some time to find the address he has given me in Central Havana; when I finally do, he's not at home, so I wait. The street is typical of many in the area: the road surface is heavily scarred with potholes, and some of the buildings have collapsed into rubble, leaving behind an imprint, tattoo-like, of each room on the walls of its neighbours that still stand. On one building a set of stairs runs intact along a wall and up into a bedroom which no longer exists.

Roberto turns into the street. As I watch him approach I wish I had a camera to capture this contrast that is so dramatic: the immaculate white suit, the *babalao's* blue-black skin, and the background of crumbling 18th century colonial architecture; it's an image quintessentially Cuban. Children playing baseball pause momentarily to greet their *babalao*. Roberto is treated with the same courtesy and respect that a priest in Ireland would have been shown fifty years ago.

He's an educated man, and has devoted almost twenty years of his life to the study of Santería. Each morning he rises before dawn and studies the Book of Ifá, the key Santería text, which all *babalaos* follow for spiritual guidance. Most of his day is spent in consultation with local people who have asked for his help. Just now, for example, he was in the nearby hospital where a relative, an eight year-old-boy, is seriously ill.

"I was called to the hospital unexpectedly, when the child's condition worsened, so I didn't have time to prepare for the ritual. Under normal circumstances I would go with a dove. This morning I had nothing with me to cleanse the child, to absorb the malevolence, so the doctor was furious, and rightly so. She was very worried that, having been drawn out of the child, the negative energy would enter the body of one of the patients around him. But what could I do? He's my cousin's only son and I have to think of him first."

He welcomes me into his home. The living room is sparse. No decorative ornaments or trinkets, so beloved by Cuban women, break its sombre monotony. Everything around me is functional, except the squat figure of *Eleggua* beside the front door. Over coffee, Roberto asks if I'd like to throw the pieces of coconut shell, to obtain insights and wisdom from the *orishas*. Deisy has mentioned this to me, but she stressed that Santería only permits *babalaos* to perform this ritual, and that if I am offered the opportunity by one I should try it.

We move across the living room into a small alcove in one corner by the door. Once inside, I sit cross-legged on a cushion and Roberto draws a curtain behind us. Another *Eleggua* is positioned in the corner and on a shelf there is a statue of Saint Barbara, the Catholic symbol for *Changó*, the powerful Yoruba god of fire, thunder and lightning.

Roberto sits opposite me. Placing a beautifully bound copy of the Book of Ifá beside him he opens a small carefully folded square of cloth to reveal a set of four pieces of coconut shell. He takes them and breathes in slowly while holding the pieces firmly between both palms. As he is handing them to me he asks casually if I'm menstruating. The question has taken me by surprise and I'm too embarrassed to admit the truth. I tell a lie and hope that the *orishas* won't curse me for it. Next, he invites me to take the coconut pieces and hold them between my palms, to feel their texture, pass them from left to right, and then to throw them into the space on the floor between us. The pieces have symbols painted on them and these symbols are read in conjunction with the Book of Ifá, which Roberto opens at particular pages, according to how the coconut pieces fall. The procedure takes about half an hour and much of that time is spent with me in silence while Roberto consults the book and interprets the message.

Before I leave I ask Roberto if he can give me some advice about romance.

"You should have asked me in there," he says gesturing to the alcove. "The *orishas* were with us just now. Well, let's hope they're still listening."

"I want to make a man, a Cuban doctor, fall madly in love with me. I want him to forget every other woman but me." I try to sound tongue-in-cheek but a hint of anxiety laced the tone of my voice. Roberto grins.

"The first part is easy. You have a lot going for you and it's hard to imagine how a man could resist that. The second part is much more difficult, This is Cuba, you know."

"I was hoping for perhaps some kind of magic potion, maybe."

"An aphrodisiac? That's not what I do. There are rituals, of course, that Santería practitioners follow and if it comes to it, then I will tell you what you have to do. Right now, I sense there's no need for it. Buy a stick of cinnamon and chew it. My ex-wife and my sister swear by cinnamon-scented breath. That's the first step. Try it and let me know how it goes. "

The following day, I visit San Antonio de Padua church located in the elegant Miramar neighbourhood. Father Chasco, a Basque priest of the Franciscan order, has agreed to meet me to talk about the role of Catholicism in Santería.

"The irony," he remarks, "is that the Catholic Church has a lot to be grateful to Santería for. You can't be a *santero*, or a *babalao*, or even a practitioner of Santería unless you have been baptised. It's a prerequisite, and that's why we're so busy with the baptisms of adults. But once that's over very few ever go to mass on a regular basis."

We enter the church and he points to a beautifully ornate statue in an alcove at the front, it's Our Lady of Charity of El Cobre, the patron saint of Cuba.

"Those people kneeling there in front of her now could be praying to Our Lady of Charity or to *Oshun*, the *orisha* she represents. So complete is the syncretism that in their minds they are one and the same, Our Lady and the Santería deity for love and beauty. It's complex and to help us understand it we Franciscans were offered specialist training at the seminary on the subjects of Santería, Palo Monte, and spiritism. I don't even ask myself whether I should be concerned about our parishioners' beliefs. I endeavour always to show them respect. What matters is that people come to our church to pray. That's the most important part of all of this."

The previous week I had visited the small town of El Cobre, in the east of Cuba, and, with scores of others, filed into the large ornate church dedicated to Our Lady of Charity, or *Oshun*. Eponymously named, El Cobre is a copper-mining town, although very little mining takes place these days, since the mineral reserves are almost depleted. Many of its inhabitants now make a living by selling religious trinkets and souvenirs to vast numbers of tourists, both Cuban and foreign, who visit the town to pay homage in the church. Among the dozens of offerings on display in a large glass case in the building is the medal awarded to Ernest Hemingway when he won the Nobel Prize of Literature in 1954; alongside is the Olympic silver medal that Cuban high jumper Javier Sotomayor won in Sydney in 2000. Many other, more humble, offerings are testament to the deep devotion paid to the patron saint of Cuba.

Father Chasco is still on my mind when I turn into Calle San Francisco later that afternoon. A trailer has just drawn up outside the entrance to my building and the neighbours are unloading a goat and coaxing it up the stairs. Half a dozen initiates troop in behind it, clasping sunflowers and candles. Liliana is standing in her doorway watching with interest.

"This must be an important ceremony for a goat to be sacrificed. I wonder what's going on. Only a *babalao* can offer up the life of a hoofed animal. Anyway, come on in. I've got some good news for you," she says with a broad smile.

"While you were out, Alexis phoned twice. He was keen to know when you'd be home."

I hurry off to find my ancient mulatto with oriental features in the hope that I'll get a stick of cinnamon from him. When I arrive home the goat is dead and the chanting has ceased. It is forbidden to sound the drum in the Santería faith once darkness falls.

CHAPTER 6

Between The Frying Pan And The Fire

"*Hola* Irish woman! Great to see you. Take a seat, but we might not be able to stay here for long. They're just about to fumigate. Either the fumigations or the bats, one or the other, will be the end of me."

I have just walked into the office of Ramón López Carrillo, head of the Translations Centre at The Cuban Institute of the Book (ICL) in Old Havana to collect a cheque. Ramón often uses these words to greet me, "Irish woman." They are the only words in English he has ever spoken to me and he pronounces them with affection. Ramón is a loyal friend and colleague whose integrity, astuteness, and professionalism have won my admiration from the very start of our friendship, which began while I was still employed by *Granma*. I pull up a chair and look across the desk at this thick-set fifty-something man who appears to be even more harried than usual today. At that meeting I didn't take his concerns very seriously, but I should have done.

Shortly after I left Cuba Ramón died of respiratory failure and his family blames the bats.

Ramón has been in his office since 8.00. In summer he arrives in advance of the heat, but he is perspiring now and looks uncomfortable. Dark stains have formed around the armpits of his polyester shirt and are expanding as we speak; he is dabbing his forehead repeatedly with a limp handkerchief. The overhead fans are still and his computer screen is blank. For almost an hour, Ramón tells me, there has been no electricity and even though the power cut may last beyond lunch time, or longer, workers have to remain at their desks until they can clock off. Most of the staff resorts to translating by longhand, including Ramón, to stave off the boredom. He hands me a glass of tepid water and points to the high vaulted ceilings. I look up and see that much of the plaster is cracked and crumbling, but this is commonplace in Cuba.

"Forget the state of plaster; it's the bats I'm worried about." I look again but don't see any signs of bats.

He directs my attention to a space beyond the ancient wooden beams.

"They roost up there, a little further out, under the eaves. Either the bats or the fumigations of the mosquito brigade will kill me."

I still don't see anything but I allow him to persuade me that the gaps and crevices around the beams in the furthest recesses of the ceiling might make an inviting homestead for a colony of bats.

The publishing house where Ramón works has been based in this beautiful eighteenth-century building since the early 1980s, when moved from its location in Central Havana. Ramón has been an employee since the late 1960s but he's planning to retire early from his position and devote his time to working at home on whatever freelance translation contracts he can secure. He hopes that prolonged exposure to the bats is not going to have serious health consequences. The problem, he makes clear to me, is not the bats in themselves; it's their droppings, or more precisely, the fungus on bat excrement, or guano, that is his main concern. Guano, Ramón explains, is associated with deadly lung disease, and his lungs are already scarred from pneumonia. Just talking about the problem makes him wheeze.

He reaches into his briefcase and slides out an envelope with my name on it. We have an arrangement which requires some discretion, or perhaps furtiveness would be a better way of describing it. I pick up the cheque and walk to a nearby bank, where I cash it for dollars and divide the notes into two envelopes, Ramón's share and mine. He checks my translation work and I reimburse him out of the fee the Cuban office for tourism promotion pays me. Sometimes he accompanies me, but mostly he doesn't because his presence with me in the bank might raise an eyebrow if a colleague were to spot him accepting an envelope from a foreigner. Such is the law that under no circumstances can he receive payment in dollars for his work as a translator. Cubans are not permitted to be paid in hard currency by companies or organisations based on the island for freelance work while I, as a non national, am. There's no risk involved for me in these clandestine operations but I need to be cautious. If he is uncomfortable having to depend on me, on us foreigners, for this favour of being paid in this way, he doesn't show it.

This morning I cash the cheque and return to Ramón's office. Once the door is firmly closed I hand him the envelope containing his share, which he hastily places in his briefcase. As I turn to leave, he tells me about the petty criminals operating in Old Havana who have resorted to Mossad-style tactics to separate foreigners from their money.

"They know that tourists tend to hide their cash in pouches worn under their clothes, so now they use commando-style speed to pull the victim's tee-shirt over their head, momentarily blindfolding them with it, and slash the purse strings. It takes three seconds. Then they're gone."

It's sinister, but I laugh.

"Mine is going into a money belt inside my knickers."

He beams back at me,

"Very smart, Irish woman. That's one place only you have the lock and key to!"

In the passage outside Ramón's office it's cooler. The oyster-white marble floor is well over a century old and it's cracked and scuffed now with age. In colonial times, elegant Creole ladies, fans in hand, would have glided across, closely followed by slaves bearing trays of sliced papaya and tropical beverages. At the top of the broad stone staircase sweeping down into the colonial courtyard I pause to imagine how it must have been on the night of lavish balls here, when all eyes from below turned to gaze at the costumed beauties descending into the opulent gathering. Except for a few indigent plants and a brown-uniformed security guard, the courtyard is empty now. The guard calls out to me as I'm crossing the courtyard and when I turn she reaches into her pocket for my identity card, which all visitors are obliged to hand over on entering the building as a precaution against an unnamed threat. I thank her and pass through the archway onto the cobblestones of the plaza, where a wall of heat awaits me, thick and oppressive even though it is only 9.30 am.

On the corner, where Plaza de Armas and O'Reilly Street meet, there's a plaque high on the wall that I occasionally stop to read. In three languages, English, Spanish and Gaelic, it speaks of:

Two island people

In the same sea of struggle and hope

Cuba and Ireland

According to local tour guides, O'Reilly fought in the war of independence against the Spanish back in the nineteenth century. They say he was a wealthy landowner of Irish descent but have no further knowledge of him. When I ask what else they know about Ireland, they look blank, shamefaced that they cannot tell me more. When it comes to their own country though, these guides' familiarity with every detail is staggering. Much of what I've learnt about Cuban history, politics and the economy, I've picked up from the tour guides who I work with from time to time. This morning when I glance up at the plaque, I see it has been sun bleached to the extent that the words have faded into barely legible imprints on ash-grey stone.

Some bicycle taxi (also known as Pedicabs or bicycle rickshaw) owners are parked nearby and one calls out to me in heavily accented English, "I'll carry you wherever you want, for ten dollars. Special price for a lovely lady."

It's extortionate but I'm not in the mood so I smile and decline politely. His smile wilts and he looks defeated, vulnerable. With so few tourists around in the mid-summer heat, he'll be lucky if he scoops more than a couple of dollar-paying passengers today. When I glance back he's laughing with some of his friends, the momentary disappointment forgotten.

A number of the Pedicab drivers that I have spoken to have university degrees, and may have spent some time working in their chosen professions before deciding to apply for a dollar income self-employment licence. Dollars pay the bills, pesos do not. It's the consideration that must be foremost in their minds when they lower themselves onto the driver's seat for the first time and start hustling for passengers. But licences are increasingly difficult to obtain and consequently, with a spirit of creativity and enterprise, most Cubans decide to do two jobs, their day job in the state sector and an unsanctioned evening job, which rarely has any connection with their official employment. Doctors make and repair shoes. Engineers give massages. Hairdressers bake and sell cakes. Bus drivers raise pigs. Teachers take in laundry. Psychologists become nocturnal seamstresses.

All of this is about generating extra income; it is what Cubans call *por la izquierda*, literally via the left. It's illegal, forming part of the black market, a vast parallel economy extending into practically every area of life. Virtually anything that is purchased, goods or services, can be found cheaper *por la izquierda*. Indeed, a many items not available in shops can be procured on the black market, Mp3 players, memory sticks, fake designer sunglasses, video recorders, spare parts for car engines.... It would be a challenge to find a single family that does not rely in some way on the black market.

In Ramón's case, it is because he wants to work as a translator that the authorities will not grant him a self-employed licence. Competition with a government-paid job which the state has trained him for is not permissible. He feels he has no option but to do a gruelling double shift, which is what so many other Cubans do. Every evening he sets off from his office, where he is paid in Cuban pesos, at just a fraction of what he earns on his "evening shift." He cycles to his home in Cerro, freewheeling part of the way, and zigzagging the rest of it to avoid the numerous potholes that ravage the surface of Calle Monte. The journey takes about twenty-five minutes but the heat, and the hazards caused by anarchic bus and taxi drivers constantly cutting in front of him are draining, and Ramón arrives home drenched in sweat and exhausted. Commuting would be much easier if he used his mud-coloured 1970s Lada, but a shortage of spare parts, and a lack of cash to pay for them, has forced the car off the road for the past year. In any case, the daily outlay on fuel alone would rapidly consume an entire peso salary.

After a shower and his evening meal, Ramón sits down with his Russian wife Tatiana at the computer in their study and begins the work that pays in hard currency, in dollars. They translate books into Spanish for foreign publishers, mostly Mexican and Spanish contracts that Ramón has secured through contacts he has made over the years. He and Tatiana are highly competent and astonishingly prolific, having translated well over a hundred works of fiction and non-fiction between them, on a wide range of topics. They are dedicated professionals whose income from their linguistic skills in French, Russian, Italian, Portuguese and English has to remain "discreet."

When husband and wife are not translating books, they revise tourist information brochures and publications that we native speakers translate from Spanish into our own languages for Cuban organisations on a freelance basis. It is poorly paid, at only five dollars a page, but I'm grateful for the work and, together with the dollars I earn as a tour leader, it is my main source of income after leaving *Granma International*. Ramón's knowledge of English and the other languages he works with is highly detailed, allowing him to pick up on the mistakes in the translations we hand over to him. Every sentence is rigorously revised and compared with the original to ensure that the texts mirror each other. Tatiana reads the Spanish version aloud while Ramón scours the translation for any deviation. It is a mind-numbingly tedious process because the original Spanish version is frequently little more than page upon page of nauseating verbiage which translators must remain loyal to, though we may squirm and thump the desk in despair at what we read. Cuba has so much to offer visitors and yet nothing that I translate ever conveys the magic of the island or its people. Vibrant and sparkling journalism, it most certainly is not. This is Ramón's life, night after night, a rhythm interrupted only by power cuts or illness.

Ramón's dream is to visit his homeland, Galicia in the north west of Spain. Nostalgia softens his tone when he talks about it and yet he has never been there. He means his spiritual homeland, for he is a second-generation immigrant who regards having been born in Havana almost as an accident. In his heart and mind he is *gallego,* Galician, the term that Cubans use when they mean Spanish. Fidel Castro is frequently referred to as *gallego,* of Spanish descent.

With his white skin, slightly bronzed from exposure to the sun on his bike rides to work, straight hair and stocky frame, Ramón is much more European than Caribbean. That he has married a Russian woman, and not a temperamental *mulatta*, is unsurprising. Tatiana, originally from Leningrad/St. Petersburg, arrived in Havana in the late 1960s as a recent addition to the pool of Russian-Spanish-French translators at the publishing house. Of Jewish descent, she is taciturn in every regard except where her pets, particularly her dog, is concerned. She lavishes attention on Fred, a cantankerous daschund that sleeps in her bed at night and sits by her feet during the day while she works on the computer. When she rises from her desk, Fred rises too, wriggling, worm-like, to heave his stocky little body onto his feet and accompany her. I despise the sound of his nails click-clicking on the tiled floor as he struggles to keep pace with Tatiana and I know the feeling is mutual. When he click-clicks into the room, I reach instinctively for my left eye, fingering the small scar where his teeth penetrated the skin one summer evening. I'm not the only family friend that Fred has bitten, although the attack on me was particularly vicious. Tatiana refuses to get rid of the dog.

"I need some advice, Tatiana."

She pauses at the keyboard and looks across at me.

"What kind of advice?"

"Things aren't working out for me in Liliana's house."

Liliana is a close neighbour and it was on Ramón and Tatiana's recommendation that I approached her when I was looking for accommodation. I confide that for the first couple of months everything went quite smoothly and then Yanelis, Liliana's nineteen-year-old grand niece, moved in with her mother. The move was supposed to be temporary but she seems to have settled in.

"The house is overcrowded. It's too small for four women. Yanelis and her mother were never part of the agreement and … the truth is she's been stealing from me."

"Mother of God! How do you know?"

Yet before I can respond Tatiana asserts that she should have suspected as much because Yanelis has been seen getting into rented cars and hanging out with foreigners.

"She's going to end up as a prostitute, if she's not already working as one. She's not to be trusted."

I'm shocked by the frankness of her assertion but ignore it and answer her question. It was Liliana herself who found out about the thefts. She came into my bedroom one afternoon clutching some of my clothes and a few toiletries, which she'd found secreted amongst Yanelis' belongings. After placing them on my bed, she told me I should consider getting a lock put on my bedroom door. I'd never seen her looking so despondent. That was over a month ago but the thefts have continued and now each time I leave the house I feel uneasy, suspicious as to whether Yanelis is taking advantage of my absence to raid my room. I'm not going to get a lock; I refuse to live in the same house as a woman who is stealing from me. My inclination is to look for alternative accommodation but Tatiana suggests I give her an opportunity to talk to Liliana first.

"Give her a chance to remedy this. She really needs your rent and if you leave her financial situation will be disastrous."

I agree, partly because I don't want to be responsible for depriving Liliana of income which she is clearly dependent on, but also because I find the mere thought of the bureaucratic obstacles I will have to clear when I register another change of address wearying.

For the next hour or so I try not to worry about Yanelis and the thefts while we sip iced black tea and chat. Tea, not espresso coffee, is the preferred refreshment in Ramón's home. We are drinking it because Tatiana, as an émigré, has right of access to the exclusive Russian shop located in the residential Vedado neighbourhood of the city. Almost every Saturday the couple goes there in search of items that are not available on the open market, like tea, potted herring and Black Sea caviar. With Tatiana by his side, Ramón is permitted to enter the premises as her husband. Without her, the security guard would probably turn him away.

The Russian shop is one of a number of retailers in the city that serve only ex-pats or foreigners. Others include the *diplo tienda* in the élite Miramar neighbourhood, where only diplomats may shop. This exclusiveness extends to hotel chains across the island which will not rent a room to a Cuban, no matter how much money they offer to pay. It is against the law.

Intrigued to see what this "exclusive" shop might be like and what it sells, I ask Tatiana for directions and set out to find it with "my" Cuban doctor, Alexis in tow. We circle and back track a couple of times on the bike, confused because we cannot see any shops at all on the block she has directed me to in Vedado. All the buildings are elegant magnolia, white and pastel pink nineteenth- and early twentieth-century mansions, either residences or government offices, ensconced behind high fences and abundant vegetation. Baffled and uncomfortably hot, we approach a security guard who is dawdling by the gate of one of these stylish buildings. He replies that the Russian shop is on the premises behind him, at the end of the long narrow passage beside the garden, leading to the rear of the mansion. After inspecting my ID, he nods his assent. Turning to Alexis, the guard stresses that as a Cuban he will have to wait outside, in the street, and closes the gate behind me. I'm embarrassed by the "privileges" accorded to me but enter anyway, promising to be only be a few minutes, a promise which the security guard underscores.

"It's closing for lunch at midday anyway."

I check my watch and it's quarter to the hour, so I hasten down the passage, cross the rear patio and enter. From the bright sunshine I pass into musty semi-darkness, all the wooden shutters are closed, but shafts of light pierce the louvre slats and illuminate the room in an uneven fashion. It resembles an early twentieth-century parlour more than a shop. Three or four people are shuffling around, and after my eyes adjust I see that one of them is an assistant, apparently Russian, with razor-sharp cheekbones, ice-blue eyes and blonde hair pulled back into a tight bun. She's lifting boxes from an elegant *chaise-longue* by the window on to the counter. Behind her are ceiling-high shelves stacked with tins, all labelled in Russian. The couple she is serving is deliberating over an impressive display of liquor, vodka presumably; the wife moves effortlessly between her own language and Spanish, spoken in a Havana accent that betrays her Russian origins only now and again.

Behind me there is a rack of clothes, a bizarre selection of oversized fur coats. Mittens, satin evening dresses, paisley-design polyester blouses, plastic high-heeled shoes, and some costume jewellery; none of it is fashionable. There is very little to interest a Cuban here, unless they were planning to travel to Russia, but those days are long gone. Student and professional exchanges ended in the early 1990s when the Soviet Union collapsed. I am effectively looking at relics. I turn to the shop assistant.

"What's in the tins?"

Blondie looks at me. Glares at me.

"It's the labels. Sorry, but I can't understand Russian."

Stiffly, like a cat arching its back in fury, she turns away from me to face the wall of tins, sighs, and then, turning to glare at me again, asks in measured tones if I think she has time to read the labels of all the stock.

Her attitude stinks. Antipathy toward customers is commonplace among shop assistants in Havana, whether they are Cuban or not. What I also register is her facial expression, tone and gestures, which are identical to her Cuban counterparts. Momentarily I wonder whether the Russians imported their techniques for dealing with the public when they first arrived on the island back in the 1970s or whether Cubans "contaminated" them. Which was it? Then the security guard calls time. He rounds us up and herds us out of the door, sharpish. I leave empty-handed, without the black tea I promised to buy Ramón. Outside, Alexis remains impassive while he listens to me rant. Our little excursion has ended in disappointment and he shrugs his shoulders,

"That's the way we live, the way we have to live, a constant struggle for something as simple as tea."

Over coffee the following afternoon, conversation in Ramón's house drifts from complaints about the state of the economy to politics. Political opinions vary significantly among the families I know in Cuba. Some are – in private - bitterly hostile and oppose Fidel Castro's government, while others shrug in resignation or acquiescence. None are sycophantic supporters of the kind who appear daily on television or in public at mass meetings held to denounce one or other aspect of foreign aggression. Ramón says he prefers not to waste time thinking or talking about politics, arguing that a lifetime on the island has taught him it is fruitless to hope for change for the better. This government and this economic system is all he has known, for the revolution took place when he was barely a toddler.

"Hope," he says, "can lead to disappointment, and disappointment, to bitterness. It's not in my nature to be bitter, so I keep out of politics." Nevertheless, when the "idiosyncrasies" of the government, as he calls them, disturb his equanimity, he can launch into an angry denunciation that leaves his hands trembling.

The idiosyncrasy which has riled him on this occasion is a nationwide campaign by the authorities calling on people to sign a government petition in favour of constitutional change. If successful, as it undoubtedly will be, the socialist nature of the Cuban state will be made permanent, or "untouchable," according to the wording of the proposal. Few of the eight million who sign are fully aware of the circumstances which gave birth to the petition. Ramón is. He knows that it is directly linked to another (earlier) petition, known as the Varela Project, signed by just over 11,000 Cubans and presented to the Cuban parliament in May 2002.

The Varela Project was a risky and potentially subversive initiative calling for legislation overhaul in very delicate matters, including greater freedom of expression and association, an amnesty for political prisoners, the opening of the market to private initiatives, and for electoral reform. All in all, there were twenty proposals for far-reaching changes that represented a challenge to the status quo. The threat was double-edged in that, on the one hand, the law – specifically Article 88 of the 1976 Constitution – obliges parliament to debate any petitions presented to it, on the condition that they are signed by 10,000 or more vote-registered citizens. On the other hand, certain names associated with the Varela Project were known to the Cuban government as dissidents, which raised hackles in official circles even further.

Before the assembly had decided how best to deal with the petition, former U.S. president Jimmy Carter travelled to the island on what was perceived to be a historically significant goodwill visit. Recently arrived, Carter made a public speech in the University of Havana, broadcast live on Cuba television, during which he referred to the Varela Project on several occasions. Had he not done so, it is reasonable to assume that the 11,000 signatures may have been dispatched to a dusty backroom and forgotten. As it was, the words "Varela" and "Project" were on Cubans' lips everywhere in the hours and days following Carter's speech. Questions were being asked, and something had to be done.

Reaction was swift on the part of the authorities. Firstly, the nature of the proposals backed by the 11,000 signatures was obscured, appearing in summary in the *Granma* daily newspaper and presented as a call for a return to capitalism, which hardly conveyed the breadth of their aims. When that edition was sold out only those with access to the Internet could develop their grasp of what the Varela Project petition was calling for in broader terms. For the general public it was "packaged" and presented on television and in the press as an attack on socialism. So successful was media portrayal of the Varela Project that within days of Carter's speech, it was widely perceived as little more than a call for the privatisation of the economy and a return to capitalism. Secondly, having manipulated the general understanding of what the Varela Project consisted of, the state then launched its response with a counter petition – in the form of a national referendum backed by over eight million signatures demanding that socialism be made permanent. One of the first to sign was President Fidel Castro who, pen in hand, proclaimed that "Imperialist domination and capitalism will never return to Cuba."

This is what the immense majority of Cubans believed they were signing up to when they added their name to others on the referendum: they were rejecting imperialism and capitalism.

"I am signing for socialism and against Yankee interference in our affairs," says Elisa. Others, many others, agree with her and they sign too.

"But you already have socialism" I say. "What difference does it make if you sign or not? You are calling for something you already have."

She shrugs her shoulders.

"It will be forever now."

Ramón has followed events closely and is clear that the government referendum is about carpet-bombing the demands of the Varela Project.

"We've been hoodwinked from the outset. There'll be no more Varela Projects once this referendum becomes law. Ask for change peacefully, constitutionally, and they stamp on you. That's the way it always has been and the way it always will be."

"So, why are you signing, then?"

"Because I have a job I want to keep and a son at university. I want him to get his degree. I can't afford to have trouble with the authorities. At the very least, they'll take away my right of access to the Internet and it could be worse, a lot worse than that. It's not just your signature; they want your ID number too on the referendum."

He doesn't just look tired, he looks defeated.

"We've had a lifetime of this, campaign after campaign, obsession after obsession. Take the insects, for example. We're expert entomologists on this island, you know, the *thrips palmi* bug, you don't remember that, do you? Now it's the *aedes aegypti* mosquito. Every year it changes. In the beginning there was the literacy campaign, thank God I was too young to be recruited for that. Then there was the goal of the ten million ton sugar harvest, and lately Elián González, the Five Heroes, Hugo Chávez and Venezuela. And on and on it goes."

Jimmy Carter returned home to the United States and the commotion caused by his visit quickly faded from the collective memory. As for the Varela Project, it too soon passed into oblivion. Constitutional change was approved when the petition of eight million signatures was presented to the national assembly and socialism effectively became permanent, out of reach of any further independent bids for change. Once the dust had settled, scores of arrests were made in a sweep that put many of the leading figures behind the initiative in prison on a range of charges. A campaign was immediately launched, waged from abroad, to have them and other political prisoners released.

A mood of resignation and pessimism descended on those who clung to the hope that Jimmy Carter and the Varela Project might have created some kind of opening, yet I never hear even a whisper of rebellion. Fear of being overheard by state security agents is widespread. Rumours suggest that there is one in every workplace department, one on every block in the neighbourhood, maybe even one in ten adults has his or her ears open for the purpose of passing on information to their handlers. It is impossible to be one hundred per cent certain that your colleague, neighbour or even family member has not been recruited, so discretion tends to prevail in conversations touching on politics or government leaders.

Fear, however, is also tinged by a healthy dose of realism. As Ramón once put it,

"We Cubans are very conscious that we live on an island in the Caribbean which is surrounded by bankrupt and authoritarian regimes. In this context, what can we expect from change? This is not Europe and there won't be a Scandinavian-style solution for us. It will be out of the frying pan and into the fire of savage free-market capitalism. That's not an exciting prospect at all."

CHAPTER 7

Life In Jaimanitas

Tatiana is helping me pack the last of my belongings when I hear Liliana's heavy steps in the hall. She halts in the doorway and surveys the scene. Bereft of my accoutrements, the bedroom looks sallow, motes of dust hang in the air, momentarily captive in the beams of sunlight that pierce the louvre blinds.

"Jaimanitas is full of prostitutes who make a tidy living from tourists they pick up on Fifth Avenue, you'll see," she hisses.

"Liliana, I've already decided that I'm leaving here. I'm taking my chances."

We've come to the end of the line. The past fortnight has been peppered with tempestuous rows over the continuing thefts. Nothing, not even the shame of being detected and forced to apologise, has prevented Yanelis from creeping into my room and foraging when I'm out. Liliana is clearly not going to ask her grand-niece to leave the house, so I announce that I'm going. The loss of $100 rent a month will be devastating for a woman whose regular income does not amount to a tenth of that figure. I see it on her face.

"In that case, I curse you. I curse you and I curse that relationship you have started. Nothing good will come out of it. You will never be happy with Alexis."

"Liliana, that's enough!" Tatiana interrupts.

I am stunned and hurt by the viciousness of her outburst, but don't respond, enough words have already been said. Instead I shoulder one of my bags and begin dragging another toward the door, where I'll wait for Alexis in the street. He is due to collect me any minute and I don't want to remain in this poisonous atmosphere any longer.

Thankfully, Alexis arrives early and he and Tatiana load the boot of the car while I sit in the back seat staring straight ahead, willing the vehicle to move. Liliana's words sting me even as Alexis reaches for my hand and then we pull away from her house on Calle San Francisco.

Half an hour later and I'm about twenty kilometres away, in the suburb of Jaimanitas, a scattering of a few hundred homes lining a dozen or so streets, many of which lead directly to the shoreline. Jaimanitas is a former fishing village that still retains the unmistakeable personality of its origins, with row upon row of wooden houses framed by the immense backdrop of the Gulf of Mexico. Alexis switches off the engine and I step out of the car to listen to the rhythmic lapping of the waves. The tranquillity is almost palpable. Hemingway would have fallen in love with Jaimanitas, if indeed he ever made it this far west of Havana. He would have breathed the tang of fresh fish and tuned in to the irregular collective heartbeat of a colony of wooden boats bumping against the jetty where they were once moored. There are no longer any fishermen here now; Jaimanitas is more of a suburb, a place where *habanero* commuters return home to after making the journey out here from other parts of their city.

Alexis helps me unload my luggage and carry it up the steps to the porch of my new home. He doesn't stay for longer than a few minutes though; a more complex than usual neurosurgery case has been programmed for this afternoon and he is the chief anaesthetist. He looks harried and careworn.

At the sight of my three unpacked suitcases, sitting on the threshold, an aching loneliness wells up in me. I'm a long way from the busyness of the life I led in the overcrowded streets in Cerro. How will I cope so far from Elisa, and from my other friends who live in the city – from my support network? At two bus rides, Jaimanitas is further away from them than I had calculated. But then I shouldn't be lonely for long as Alexis is moving in with me at the end of the month.

This flat, with its front row view of the Gulf of Mexico, has to be the most stunning location I have ever lived in. I feel smug in the knowledge that it's the kind of setting which only millionaires have the privilege of enjoying in other parts of the world, and it is certainly a long way from my terraced street in Belfast. The rear balcony overlooks the shallow transparent waters of the sea, just six or seven metres directly below. This is the same sea that crashes into the Atlantic coast of Ireland, though by then it's a few degrees colder. To my left, looking westward, is *The Old Man and the Sea*, a hotel situated right on the coast, at the very end of the Hemingway Marina. Soon I'll see boats equipped with the tackle for marlin fishing heading out to sea from here. To the right, the coastline stretches east, in towards Havana, but just now the humidity and shimmering heat have blurred all but the most prominent landmarks. Out front, only a tiny key, less than 100 metres wide, stands between me and Florida. No matter how clear the day, there is no hint of the vast land mass out there on the horizon, beyond that key. The United States could be reached from here in an hour by car, but it remains invisible and impossible, unless you happen to build a boat you have faith in to carry you there.

Turning my back on the view, I drag my suitcases indoors and begin the task of making this space into a home that will reflect some of my personality. It's a one-bedroom flat that sits on top of Jaime and Ana's ground floor house. The flat was built for their daughter and her husband when they married five years ago. The couple are now living downstairs, with their two children and their ancient grandmother, Mirta, so there are seven people crowded into the space below me. They need the rent, which is why I have the luxury of my own place.

I'm still unpacking when Ana calls to me from the rear balcony. She's just come up the stairs with a glass of fresh *sapote* milkshake, the first of many treats she will offer me during the two years I shall remain in her daughter's home. We sit and look at the sea while Ana talks to me about herself and her family. She's planning to leave the children's nursery where she has worked for almost thirty years as the centre director. The job is very rewarding but there's no money in it, so she's taking early retirement and going to apply for a licence to work as a self-employed caterer, providing buffets for parties and takeaway meals sold from home. Her husband, Jaime, is a delivery driver for the nearby Ñico López Communist Party training school, and he too has been employed in the same workplace since his late teens. Their daughter, Anita, is a nurse in the same research hospital as Alexis, which is where she met her husband, Ernesto, a neurosurgeon.

"So, I'm living in a brain surgeon's house, then?"

For me it's bizarre, but Ana doesn't see anything out of the ordinary in it. Brain surgeons, like doctors in general, enjoy the respect of the community but in Cuba they aren't necessarily any wealthier than Mr Average. She replies that Anita and Ernesto will be saving the rent I pay them so that they can build an extension to the front of the house.

"The flat is too small for four of them. If we buy the building materials with the rent money and do the construction work ourselves, we'll make it into a decent-sized home, instead of a rabbit hutch."

Ana is full of plans and brimming with energy, as well as being incredibly multi-skilled. She's willing to mix sand and cement, put up plaster, paint, cook, sew and clean – whatever it takes to improve her and her family's lives. It is from her that I often hear a very Cuban phrase, *sigo en la lucha* (I'm still in the struggle) whenever I ask how she is getting on. And she always says those words with a note of triumph in her voice.

"I never give up. No matter how many difficulties I encounter, I never lose sight of my goal. As the Cuban national hero and poet José Martí says, 'The measure of a man is not in the number of times he falls, but in the number of times he gets up.'"

Her stamina astonishes me. In the evenings, after arriving home from work, she and Jaime cook and sell takeaway spaghetti Bolognese to anyone from the neighbourhood who will buy. Her reputation as a good cook must have spread because on some nights there are up to a dozen people sitting in her living room watching television, or lounging around on the front porch, while their meal is being prepared in the rear kitchen. At weekends Ana cleans my flat and bakes cakes for children's parties. The only evening when she's not in the kitchen is Wednesday, when she goes to reflexology class.

In Jaimanitas I regain the independence and privacy that I lacked in Liliana's house. Having this space entirely to myself feels luxurious. I no longer have to share a bathroom with two other women or pass through the family living room when I arrive home. More importantly, the sickening suspicion that somebody might be fingering my belongings while I'm out fades. After a while I no longer think of Liliana or Yanelis, except when I'm in the area visiting Tatiana, which is when I dread crossing paths with either of them.

As the months go by, I get to know Ana and her family better. Ernesto and Anita leave for work early in the morning and return around sunset. As medical staff at a research hospital they are required to work a six-day week. Ernesto is in his mid-thirties and has already achieved some recognition for his work to the extent that he has given papers at international conferences in a couple of Central American countries. Anita is Ernesto's third wife. His first lives in his home town of Cienfuegos, on the Caribbean coast, with his eldest son, Ernesto. His second wife and second son are much closer, in a flat in Central Havana. Anita gave birth to a child, her first and his third, a girl, two years after they met. It is not unusual for men to have a number of families in Cuba, indeed, it is fairly commonplace. The problems arise when the man slyly attempts to juggle two or three families at the same time, hoping that each of them will remain ignorant of the others' existence. Inevitably, the families do generally find out about each other, although it may take months or years. This is not Ernesto's case. Anita is aware of and is on speaking terms with his previous wives. The sons often come to spend time in Jaimanitas, particularly over the summer period.

Juggling the finances is perhaps every bit as delicate as juggling emotions. Child maintenance has to be paid in Cuba, it's a legal requirement. Ernesto, as a doctor, enjoys certain benefits which he readily passes on to his families. Foreign patients treated at the hospital frequently leave generous tips or gifts for medical staff. Unwanted gifts can be sold off for cash and if the item is not easily available on the island might be worth many times more than the average monthly salary. Cuban patients, much less solvent than their foreign counterparts, know the score. A gift from them, even a modest one, wins favour and helps ensure that a doctor will perhaps remember their name in case of future necessity. This is the way things work.

This evening Ernesto is unloading a leg of pork from the boot of his Lada car. It's wrapped in torn and blood-stained newspaper, in *Granma*. He laughs mockingly when I turn my nose up.

"You vegetarians don't appreciate black bean stew flavoured with tender cuts of pork."

"How did you manage to get it out of the hospital and into your car? Weren't you worried about being seen?"

He tells me that security is on his side.

"They know I'm good at what I do and they might need me one day. In any case, I always slip them a cut of something or other, a few pounds of pork or some perfume for their wives or girlfriends. It means a lot."

Ernesto tells me that he has had a bad day. A colleague of his, another neurosurgeon, has gone to Mexico and is not coming back. Miguel was sent to an international conference in Guadalajara to give a paper the previous week and has taken advantage of the trip to defect.

"So now you have no partner in the operating theatre?"

"True. But that's not the problem. The problem is that when we opened Miguel's cubicle this morning we found a bottle of wine in there with a farewell note, telling us to drink a toast to his health, his happiness and his new life. A few of us did just that for a laugh, at lunchtime. Then, somehow or other, Julio, the hospital director, found out. We were warned that he was coming over to check for himself, to see whether the wine had been drunk. I had to get into the car and race down to the Palco supermarket and buy a replacement. Luckily, I just about managed to get back in time. Julio went berserk when he saw the note but he would have gone ballistic had there been no wine there with it."

Alexis has mentioned Julio on several occasions. He claims he's a tyrant with a furious temper who has humiliated even the most accomplished professionals on his staff with a vicious tongue lashing. Dr. Miguel is the fifth neurosurgeon to defect in the past. It was fortunate they got a tip-off, he says; otherwise there would have been hell to pay. The previous year Julio withheld the twice-yearly bonus of $70.00, paid to all surgical staff, as punishment for an unsatisfactory inspector's report. Today, Julio announced the suspension of all trips to international events until further notice. Ernesto has an invitation to attend an international conference in Chile next month, so there is a question mark over that now. He has been on a number of foreign trips before and has always returned, which goes in his favour. He has no plans to defect, as far as I know, but he was counting on the gifts that are usually bestowed upon Cuban doctors by their comparatively wealthy counterparts when they travel abroad. On his last trip to Mexico, Ernesto returned with eighty kilos of excess baggage, presents and transport all paid for by an El Salvadoran colleague.

Elite members of the Communist Party are often treated in Ernesto's hospital, if their condition is neurological or indeed if they have requested aesthetic surgery. This is the other service offered by the research hospital. A small but steady number of foreign patients, and a few Cubans, have plastic surgery here. Leaflets and the hospital website advertise everything from tummy tucks and facelifts to breast implants, as long as the patient takes responsibility for acquiring the implants, which are not available in Cuba. The surgeons are highly competent; one was trained in Brazil by a leading international specialist Dr. Ivo Pitanguy. She is no longer there and her successors, like some of the neurosurgeons, have defected when the opportunity arose. Presumably they are now earning a substantial income in Europe. The last one to hold the post is Dr. Roberto.

Dr. Roberto is from the east of Cuba and trained in the Hermanos Ameijeiras Hospital in Central Havana as a reconstructive surgeon. He quickly becomes friendly with Alexis and we invite him around to the flat in Jaimanitas a few evenings for *a Cuba Libre* rum and coke, *Tropicola*. What most attracted him to the job in the research hospital was the hospital's outstanding reputation, although he admits that the twice-yearly bonus was equally attractive. After just six months he finds himself without a job. Roberto tells us that he didn't leave voluntarily; he believes he was "set up" by the hospital management. A Mexican woman came to him for a consultation about the possibility of a face lift and a tummy tuck. When he quoted her a price she appeared to be appalled, claiming it was beyond her budget. In order to help, Roberto suggested that he invoice her for a slightly less complex procedure, obviously at a lower price. She appeared to be satisfied with this proposal and thanked him profusely. Later that afternoon Roberto was summoned to Julio's office and told to hand over his white coat and pack up his belongings. He was out and should consider himself lucky that he wasn't facing an accusation of fraud.

"That woman was probably a state security agent, briefed into laying a trap for me. I took pity on her and fell for it. They've no doubt been watching me all along, scheming to catch me out."

Six months later Alexis receives an email from Roberto telling him that he is living and working as a surgeon in Mexico City. He writes that he managed to leave the country on a passport which he acquired with a Cuban identity card that registered his occupation as a technician. As a "technician" his application for permission to travel abroad was approved. Had it stated his true profession, he would very possibly still be jobless in Havana.

Not everyone is able to bribe government officials to alter the profession on their identity card. Others have to resort to more hazardous means of fleeing the island. Early one Saturday morning, Ana stops mopping the floor of my living room and calls to me.

"Quick. Look over at Hilario's house, the police are out. Someone tipped them off about a boat."

I put down my espresso, wipe my hands and rush out to the porch. Two police cars are parked in the street, lights flashing, sirens silent. Four officers in dark blue uniforms are milling around in the front garden of a house three doors away. One is radioing through to base. A small crowd is forming on the wasteland opposite, even though it is only just past sunrise. There is no boat to be seen. I'm wondering if I have heard Ana correctly, when two of the officers advance toward the pig shed and raise a canopy covering the entrance. They peer in and signal to their colleagues to come forward. All four of them vanish into the interior for a couple of minutes, and then they haul the boat out into the back yard.

This is the first time, outside a television screen, that I have seen one of the notorious *balsas*. It's about four metres in length, quite sturdy-looking, but obviously built by amateurs. Some kind of material has been tacked on to its exterior, to waterproof it presumably, in a way that reminds of me of the *currach*, a traditional Irish seagoing vessel. Rustic oars are laid across a few beer crates arranged in the belly of the boat, presumably to serve as seats. There is a mast in there too, wrapped in a vividly coloured cloth, and even home-made life jackets. It looks like they were ready to leave. Ana looks across at me and says that this time of the year, early December, is favoured by Cubans desperate to make the crossing to Florida. In winter there are no hurricanes and the sun is less punishing. Sharks, however, remain as hungry as ever, whatever the season. As I look at the boat, it's not difficult to imagine it being bumped by three metre-long sharks, circling in a frenzied determination to make a meal of the occupants somewhere out in the Gulf of Mexico.

The boat is towed away that same day while Hilario looks on forlornly from the front garden of his house. His creation rumbles down the main street of Jaimanitas on the back of a trailer, a wounded beached turtle, a dream that seems pathetic now that it has been discovered and is on display. When the trailer finally disappears around the corner Hilario returns to the life he was planning to abandon forever. That night he enjoys a few games of dominoes with his pals on the front porch, and the following day he resumes work as a self-employed mechanic on a 1950s Buick that a client has parked behind his own beaten up Lada.

In the weeks following the decommissioning of his boat, I spy on Hilario in my moments of boredom from my rear balcony. Often he leans on the wall of his backyard, staring out to sea, wondering perhaps what that voyage would have been like and how it might have ended. Then he turns his attention to the new occupant of the shed, a pig he has called Gustavo.

Gustavo was not much larger than a puppy when he first arrived, but after just a few months he is able to stand on his hind legs and rest his trotters on the side of the sty, much as a customer at a pub might do while waiting to be served a pint of beer. The routine is always the same. Hilario approaches the sty and on hearing his footsteps Gustavo squeals with delight in anticipation of his meal. After a few words of affection, Hilario tips in the swill and listens while the pig squeaks and grunts with pleasure. Later, just after sunset, Hilario often wanders out to the sty for a quiet smoke, and I see him lean over into the gloom and pat the hairy pink back, speaking in soothing tones all the while. When this happens Gustavo's grunts turn to a contented rhythmic snuffling.

Early one morning I'm woken by the crackling of burning wood and raised voices. I peer out from behind the bedroom blinds. A fire is burning in the corner of Hilario's yard and a large blackened cauldron of water is suspended over it. Three men, including Hilario, are busy sharpening knives. A subdued grunting is coming from the pig sty behind them. The three dogs, a Jack Russell and two terrier-type mongrels, are sniffing around the yard, moving in excited circles. The westward breeze wafts tendrils of smoke in my direction, and the smell is redolent of oil. I begin to wonder what the smell of blood will be like.

All the windows in my flat overlooks Hilario's place and, unless I leave soon, I'm going to be witness to the slaughter. As a lifelong vegetarian, I suspect that I'm more squeamish than the average person. But I'm also curious by nature, and the unfolding scene has awoken my curiosity about the macabre. I can't decide what to do.

Hilario walks over to the cauldron of water and jabs it a couple of times with a stick. It's bubbling and sparks are flying from the burning wood. An ochre light bathes the scene now as the first rays of the rising sun gain in strength.

"It's time."

The others disappear into the sty. There is grunting and squealing, a curse and the sound of a slap.

Two of the dogs give excited yelps while spinning around in circles; the third watches silently, ears on the alert. A few moments later and both men haul Gustavo out of the sty and into the light. He is much larger than I had imagined, possibly weighing seventy kilos, movement is cumbersome and ungainly, and he's not cooperating. Gustavo is trying to sit, using the weight of his rear end to anchor himself to the ground. When one of the men gives him a kick. Hilario protests.

"Enough! For the love of God."

"Gimme the rope," he barks back at Hilario.

The rope is looped around Gustavo's neck and a tug of war begins.

The animal senses something horrific is about to happen. Terror has seized him and he's squealing loudly, louder than I've ever heard before. It's an ugly piercing cry that makes me put both hands over my ears and rush for the CD player. Even with the volume on full I can still hear the cacophony. A feeling of guilt washes over me and I turn the music down and walk out on to the balcony, suddenly convinced that it would be right to witness the death, as an act of homage to the life that is about to end. I stare, transfixed, as the knife-wielding man approaches the pig. His partner yanks the rope upward, exposing the soft pink throat and chest area. The dogs are yelping frenziedly now. Hilario is nowhere to be seen. The squeals are incessant, with hardly a pause between one and the next. I can't watch. I quickly step back into my kitchen, slam the door and turn up the volume of the CD player again.

When I take my hands off my ears, only the muted yapping of the dogs can be heard. Soon, the dank heavy odour of blood invades the flat, making me wretch.

Almost an hour passes before I can summon the courage to walk back out on to the balcony. When I do, Hilario is swilling the floor of his yard with buckets of water, washing rivers of blood into the sea below. The dogs are lapping up any undiluted pools still around, but he swishes them away with his brush. A table has been placed in the centre of the yard and the two men are leaning over it, each one pouring a tankard of boiling water on to the carcass and meticulously shaving the bristly white hair away from the pink skin. So gentle are their movements, in this, the first stage of making pork scratching, that it looks like an act of love.

The carving and cutting continues for the remainder of the day. Tumblers of rum are passed around, barefooted women slice and package long strips of pork, scraps are thrown to the dogs that spin around in excitement, still intoxicated by the smell of death. Afternoon fades into evening and heavy plates of pork scratching are served up together with more rum, to the accompaniment of loud salsa music and laughter.

Late the following morning, Hilario arrives with a squealing piglet tucked under his left arm. He tickles its ears and lowers it into the darkness of the sty.

On Sunday afternoon Ana sidles up to me and whispers conspiratorially that Hilario has a new wife.

"Well, not actually new, she's on trial."

This disclosure has been made with a smirk.

"On trial?"

"It's a trial run. They've brought her from the east, to see if it works out."

To have a woman on a trial basis, I am told, is quite common among people from the east of the country.

The following day I see the lady in question. She's slim, delicately framed and light-footed for her age: she must be around thirty and keeps herself busy cooking, washing and sweeping. Often I see her sitting at the table in front of the sty in the backyard, picking tiny stones from the rice grains. Ana tells me that Oriental women, as they are known, have a reputation for being hard-working and less fiery than their Havana counterparts, in other words, more submissive. Nevertheless, she doesn't stay for more than a couple of months in Jaimanitas and I surmise that the trial can't have been a success. When she's gone, all curiosity ceases. Nobody mentions her again.

Ana somehow finds time in her own busy routine to chat to me once or twice a week. One Friday evening, we sit drinking one of her specialities, café mocha, in the porch of her house. She usually has a long journey on public transport from the children's nursery where she works in Nuevo Vedado back to Jaimanitas, but today Jaime has collected her in the works delivery lorry, so she's home earlier. Even so, Ana seems wearier than usual this evening. It turns out that the Angolan ambassador paid an official visit to her centre that afternoon. Staff and children had been preparing for the occasion for weeks, rehearsing a stage show in honour of the distinguished visitor and his entourage.

"Everything went well, the costumes looked fabulous, the children remembered their lines, the props were ready, there were no power cuts, and then one little boy decided to improvise when they got into the rowing boat. And the others joined in."

"Improvise. How?"

"He started singing solo while the kids mimicked rowing and then they all joined in."

Ana couldn't suppress her amusement any longer,

"They sang *Vamos para la Yuma*! (Let's go to the USA). I was absolutely mortified. I didn't know where to look. But the ambassador looked more embarrassed than me. I doubt whether they'll continue to sponsor us now that they've seen this."

She sighs. "It's just as well I'm retiring soon because this will be a black mark against my name now."

Ana tells me that her employment record is commendable but her earnings are supplemented by selling takeaways illicitly. The spaghetti is easy to come by, as is the tomato sauce. The cheese, I suspect, is acquired from her husband's contacts in his delivery job for the Communist Party training school. It is smooth, yellow and very creamy, the kind of cheese that I usually endeavour not to look at in the supermarket, the one with the exorbitant price. The takeaway business is going well.

"I'm glad we're so popular but the customers are too visible. It's obvious what's going on here, so if anyone from the CDR or the police see them we'll be in trouble."

Which is why the queue is invited into the living room to watch TV while they are waiting for the spaghetti bolognese. It's safer that way, more discreet. Ana and Jaime's luck holds out for almost four months and then the police pay her a visit.

"Someone has reported that you are running an illegal business here, a restaurant."

Fortunately, there are no customers in her home when the police arrive. Ana tells me that she decided to brazen it out and deny the accusation. The officers take a few notes and nothing further is said. But she is so panicked that she stops selling takeaways for six months. A few weeks after she starts up the business again, there is a police raid. This time she's caught *in flagante delicto*, for there's too much spaghetti in the cauldron for the family to consume alone. Besides, as the police arrived, a party of four had just left with eight Tupperware dishes oozing Bolognese and a dozen cans of *Crystal* beer (a recent diversification). There is a hearing and Ana is fined $500 USD.

This is the real reason the family want to rent the upstairs flat to me for a further year. They can't pay the fine. Yet my presence represents another step along a treacherous path because they are renting illegally to me. If they had followed procedure, Ana and Jaime would have had to apply for a licence, requiring a hefty fee in hard currency, and also commit to paying taxes – up front – every month for a minimum period of a year, irrespective of whether they have a tenant or not. The financial risk is too daunting and they have decided to rent illegally, which could lead to their home being confiscated, if my presence is detected. I finally understand why Ana has problems sleeping at night.

Conscious of the penalty Ana and her family might incur if the authorities discover I am renting from them, I don't inform the Ministry of Foreign Affairs functionaries at the Press Centre (CPI) of my new address, which I am legally obliged to do. According to their records, and according to my identity card, I am still living with Liliana in Cerro. However, the mismatch between the landline number I use, which begins with 2 (clearly denoting Jaimanitas), and the Cerro address where I am supposed to be living, must arouse suspicion. Each time someone from the CPI phones me at home, my blood turns cold with fear, and yet, if anyone does suspect, nobody pursues the matter, which is very fortunate for me and for Ana.

That I am a foreign journalist living in Cuba and registered at a false address is an ongoing worry, but I have no choice. To rent legally is very expensive, much more than I can afford to pay.

Nevertheless, I stay where I am. I've grown very fond of my little flat, of Ana and her family and the long lazy days that seem to swaddle the passing of time in Jaimanitas. But Ana's insomnia gets worse, much worse.

"I rarely sleep soundly, and when I do, I dream of another police raid. How can I explain you away? You're a foreign journalist!"

So I pack my bags and Alexis's things and slide them across the front porch, into my next door neighbour's house. It's a two-bedroom flat that Sonia and her husband Rafael share with Sonia's elderly mother, Rosita. All three move downstairs into the spacious home of Miriam, who has been their close friend and neighbour for thirty-five years. So strong is the bond of friendship between Miriam and the family of three that they are content to live together in the same house, so content that when I eventually leave Jaimanitas, the upstairs flat that they rented to me remains vacant. All of them continue to live in the downstairs house, which they share with about half a dozen cats and Dinky, Miriam's colossal Rottweiler.

It takes me about a year to finally trust Miriam and Rafael in their reassurances that Dinky is harmless. His head is the size of a football and the ground trembles when he thunders across the porch and into the driveway to greet callers, who have to be coaxed in through the gate. In spite of his incredible bulk, he is extremely fast, particularly where the guinea fowl are concerned.

Six guinea fowl, five hens and a cock, have just moved into a fenced enclosure Rafael has built in Miriam's driveway. They have joined half a dozen hens, who are old-timers, and appear to be settling comfortably into their new community. Rafael and Sonia, who are both sugar-refinery engineers, bought them in the hope of making some extra money from the sale of guinea fowl eggs.

Within days of their arrival, it becomes apparent that Dinky has developed an infatuation with the guinea fowl. Every morning, after breakfast, he unfailingly takes up his sentry position by the pen, and from here he ogles, doe-eyed, every move the birds make, drooling and panting alternately. Only when the sun is high and no shade is available, does he surrender and slope reluctantly indoors. Should the birds alert him with that harsh discordant call of theirs, Dinky charges out of the house, seemingly prepared to use all of his seventy kilos to defend them from a presumed attack.

As the days go by, the birds become accustomed to Dinky's presence and stop shuffling defensively to the other side of the pen each time he approaches. There are many occasions when only a few inches and the all important wire fence separate the fowl from Dinky's powerful jaws. Miriam laughs about this bizarre courtship; it's the first time in the five years she has had Dinky, that there is a serious rival for his attention. Not even the three bitches they introduced him to have entranced him the way the guinea fowl do.

"Anyway, he was too heavy, too fat for them. Every time he mounted, their hindquarters gave way. It's so frustrating. The only way he'll become a father is by going on a strict diet, so as not to flatten the ladies."

I begin to suspect that sexual frustration explains this creepy obsession with the guinea fowl. A few days later the worst happens and my suspicions are partly confirmed. In his rush not to be late for work one morning, Rafael failed to secure the gate to the enclosure. By lunchtime, four of the guinea fowl are dead, but the hens inexplicably survive. On hearing the cacophony, Miriam and Sonia rush out and halt the massacre just in time to save the remaining birds, a cock and hen.

Later they tell a dismayed Rafael: "He only wanted to play with them. The harder they flapped and the louder their cry, the more excited he became."

Then they turn to me: "It was the same with the kittens. He killed three six-week-old kittens because he liked the sound of their squeaking."

If Dinky had been a man, I wonder what his sexual preference would have been. Undoubtedly something with a violent edge to it. I shudder.

New guinea fowl are purchased, but they don't last long either. This time the culprit is not Dinky, it is Charley, Hurricane Charley. This is not my first experience of a hurricane in Cuba, but it is the worst. Others have threatened Havana, but lost momentum or changed course as they approached, usually veering north and west, up to Florida. Charley, however, is steadfast. He comes up from the Caribbean, moves into Cuban territory and devastates the Isle of Youth. He then blasts the mainland, crossing Havana with winds of 150 kilometres per hour or more. Evacuations are taking place throughout the city; buses are commandeered to move the elderly, the young, and those in particularly unsafe buildings, to more secure locations.

In the hours before Charley's arrival, I watch the people of Jaimanitas mounting a defence, securing their homes as best they can. All day long, I hear hammering, as nails are driven into planks of wood placed across windows and doors. Rooftop water tanks are lashed to the cement blocks that support them. A couple of nearby palm trees – young enough to be uprooted – are hastily chopped down. Potential missiles in hurricane force winds – loose building material, washing machines, patio furniture and plants – are brought indoors. Washing lines are taken down; pigs and goats find themselves sealed into the darkness of their pens, queues form outside the local *bodegas* for candles and for rum. The old men have been through this before, and swear the best remedy for a hurricane is *la borrachera*, to get blind drunk.

All of this frantic activity is proceeding on while the sun shines benignly on Jaimanitas and a gentle easterly breeze lifts my hair. There is no hint that the weather is about to betray all of us. I'm caught between disbelief and denial. Only the constant sound of hammering and the roar of buses evacuating people tell me that something ominous is indeed happening. Then the power supply is cut. It's a precaution. My imagination flashes me an image of live wires whipped lose by the storm, thrashing manically, like the tentacles of a deadly Portuguese Man-of-War.

With no electricity and the shutters nailed down across my windows, I have to sit outside for light. I read, but mostly I follow the activity of my neighbours. The street is empty of cars and is emptying of people. The bakery is boarded up and Lucia's goat, usually tethered to the nearby lamp post, is nowhere to be seen. Rafael has placed sheets of corrugated metal around the guinea fowl pen, lashing them to the wire with my washing line. Their cries are muffled now. And still there is no hint of Charley. I feel foolish, like the bewildered host of an elaborately prepared party, wondering whether my guests will attend. I test the wind with a saliva-wettened finger. Has it changed course? Is it any stronger? I can't remember what direction it was blowing in an hour ago. Sometimes there's not a breath stirring; I'm confused.

A couple of hours later and there is no doubt that our sinister guest is arriving. Fierce gusts race in from all directions, ushering in mud-coloured clouds that rapidly turn gun-metal grey. I don't know this sea any longer. The panorama is transformed. Gone is the innocent and predictable lapping of wavelet upon wavelet. The key has vanished beneath the water, under a furious maelstrom bearing no resemblance to any movement of water I have ever seen. The spray splashes me, leaving a taste of salt in my mouth. It's time to move indoors. From the front of the house I see objects hurtling along the street, poltergeist-like, borne by the vehemence of the wind. An umbrella flies by, somersaulting wildly. I look down at the spot where my washing machine stood, until Rafael moved it indoors a couple of hours ago, and shudder at the strength of wind capable of lifting such a weight. Rafael calls up to me. I can barely hear what he's saying.

"Go indoors! It's too dangerous to be outside now."

Alexis's only pair of good shoes is parked on the balcony and, on impulse, I stoop to pick them up. This morning he announced that he wanted to be with his parents in their home, defending it from Charley. He is rarely ever away from them and I'm beginning to wonder whether he is really living with me or not. I pause, swear, and kick the shoes carelessly to one side, leaving them to their fate.

Indoors is dark and noisy. I'm sealed in and I feel trapped. The flame of my candle is flickering wildly, threatening to vanish each time the more violent gusts penetrate my home. Thin rivulets of water – that could be rain or sea – seep in through the louvre slats and run down the walls under the windows. I take the candle into the bedroom and commandeer every towel I have, wedging them into the gaps between the slats. Now there's nothing to do but wait and keep on waiting until Charley moves on. I can't read in the semi-darkness and even if I could, the roar of the storm makes it impossible to concentrate. There's nothing I can do to kill time. I get bored. The noise intensifies as waves crash heavily onto the roof above me with frightening regularity. I imagine this wall of seawater, fifteen metres high, rising up Godzilla-like, and advancing on my refuge, devastating it in seconds.

Unable to bear the sensation of being trapped and fearful of how my imagination could turn anxiety into panic, I decide to opt out altogether. The old men are probably all drunk now and I decide to follow the same course, regardless of whether or nor it is irresponsible. I gather up my cat, Patricio, and we withdraw to the spare bedroom, the only room in the flat with no windows, and I pour myself a generous measure of Havana Club. Then I pour myself another one, and another. After a fourth, I don't remember any more.

When I open my eyes, it is still dark, but silent. I stumble out of the spare bedroom along the corridor and open the front door. There is sunlight. It's mid-morning and there are people dotted about the street, assessing the damage and collecting debris. Then I remember. The old men were right, the *borrachera* is an effective remedy for fear, but my head is pounding....

Rafael is standing in the front yard looking glum. He pronounces that three of the guinea fowl are dead.

"They were either drowned by one of the waves or battered by the corrugated iron defences I shuttered them with."

I clamber down the wooden staircase leading to the front porch to have a closer look. The remaining three guinea fowl are bunched together in one corner of the pen, subdued and morose-looking. All the hens have survived.

"Sonia is cleaning the kitchen, which was flooded early on by a wave that crashed in through the back door and swept up along the corridor. It lifted up the fridge and carried it along, like a surfer."

I glance over at Rafael. He isn't smiling.

"Dinky normally sleeps in the kitchen. Luckily, Miriam had sheltered him in her bedroom, otherwise he'd be out at sea now."

For the rest of the morning, people dismantle their defences. Planks are yanked off windows and doors, outdoor furniture repopulates patios and balconies, and Lucía's goat is put out to tether. By mid-afternoon buses are unloading evacuees, who complain of cramped conditions in the refuges. The soothing rhythm of normality prevails again in Jaimanitas, by evening friends and neighbours are gathered around, sharing anecdotes about their experience of Hurricane Charley, who is now heading along the east coast of the United States.

Over the next few days and weeks, I discover I have a greater appreciation of the tranquillity and predictability of my daily routine. Memories of Charley and my fear of what could have happened lead me to take a quiet delight in feeling safe. I sit on the balcony, drinking my coffee and staring out to sea, grateful that I didn't witness its full fury, grateful that the house remained intact. My elderly neighbours, Margarita, Viviana and Delia, who live just a few metres from the shore, have lost their roof, lifted in its entirety by a single powerful gust of wind. All they can do to protect their home from the rain is arrange plastic sheets over every piece of furniture, the beds, the wardrobes, the tables and chairs. It could take up to three months for the local CDR to coordinate structural repairs. None of the women complains, because they are grateful to have survived.

Repairs to the widespread damage caused by Hurricane Charley are still being undertaken across city, and when the government announces that it has decided to redouble its efforts to wipe out the aedes aegypti mosquito. This is an age-old battle. Back in 2002, Fidel Castro said that "there is no escape," which was effectively a declaration of war on the mosquito, a carrier for dengue fever, also known as the break-bone fever. Since then brigades of young recruits have been deployed to fumigate every neighbourhood in a country-wide campaign. Homes, workplaces, abandoned property and wasteland are periodically "stormed" by uniformed, masked and nozzle-toting pseudo-commandos, who leave behind them clouds of thick oily smoke. Even though the campaign appears to be containing the number of dengue cases, there is intense resentment at the invasion of privacy. Sonia tells me that if they hear the fumigations taking place in neighbouring homes, they close the front door and pretend to be out.

My turn for a visit comes late one Saturday afternoon. It's a time when the brigades can be confident that most people are home. I don't hear their approach because I've been listening to music through headphones. When they hammer on the door, I'm so taken aback by the force of their knock that I open. Suddenly, I'm confronted by two masked men who order me out of the flat. The roar of the diesel-powered equipment is so loud that I can't hear him, his mouth opens and closes and he gesticulates. The right thumb cocked and pointing backward, over his shoulder and out, it's clear where I have to go. My cat is hiding under the bed so I try to communicate that I need time to rescue him. But the commando has already turned away and his equipment is spewing acrid smoke. I leave, fearful of what the insecticide will do to Patricio.

I'm told not to enter the flat for half an hour after the fumigation. Five minutes is all I can wait. I hold my breath and go in search of Patricio. He's still under the bed and apparently unperturbed and unharmed. But his days with me are numbered. A month later he vanishes. I search for a couple of weeks but never see him again. Ana suspects that he has ended up in the cooking pot.

"People were starving in the worst years of the Special Period and started eating their cats. Even now some of them still eat cats. Those people on the corner openly admitted to eating their two cats. I dare you to ask them if they've seen Patricio."

The nationwide offensive against the *aedes aegypti* mosquito is only one of a number of nationwide campaigns launched by the Cuban government during my stay in the country. With Elián González back in the country, except for the usual national holidays, there is a lull in the mass mobilisations, briefly interrupted by the campaign to amend the Constitution in favour of making socialism permanent, which I've already described. Later, a new slogan is launched, *Free the Five*, in reference to five Cubans jailed in the US, accused of terrorism. Once again, there is saturation coverage in the media and regular monster marches are held in the capital, as well as other cities on the island.

Rafael, Sonia, and Ana are obliged to attend the mass rallies. They leave the house at around 4.30 am, while it is still dark, and board the buses commandeered for transporting participants. The rallies start early, before it is too hot, and end just before midday. When the speeches are over, participants file back on to the bus they arrived in as part of a work contingent or with their local CDR neighbourhood association, and return home.

Alexis had no choice but to attend today's rally. He would have been excused if he had been on duty at the hospital. He arrives home exhausted.

"Wasn't there any way at all you could bunk off?"

He shakes his head and laughs bitterly. "You've been in this country long enough to know that every angle is covered. We report when we arrive at the starting point to our works delegate, and they tick the list of those who attend. One cross too many next to my name and I'm finished. I can't stand it any longer."

I suggest that we have a drink on the Hemingway Marina that evening to discuss our plans for the future. Alexis is paranoid about spies and microphones so he refuses to risk talking about the subject indoors, and particularly not in our home.

CHAPTER 8

Manicures In The Mountains

"If two million tourists come here every year, it's by coincidence. Sheer luck, in fact. It's certainly not thanks to people like her."

Diana, the tour guide, has just emerged from the Terminal 2 building at José Martí international airport. It's her fourth attempt to find out whether the Miami flight has landed in Havana yet, or whether indeed it ever took off. We are expecting twenty-two passengers to join us on a tour due to start early tomorrow morning. Juancito, our driver, is asleep in the coach, parked in the shade a few hours ago There's no need for shade now though, because the sun has set and it is dark.

Earlier we peeped through gaps in the high wall surrounding the runway but the openings are too narrow to see what airlines have planes on the tarmac. I feel ridiculous going to such lengths to determine whether our group has arrived or not. Diana warns me not to try it again because of a possible security alert; it doesn't look good, in fact, it looks downright suspicious, she says, even if we are the trip leader and tour guide. The frustration of not knowing is compounded by the fear that if the group don't arrive this side of midnight our entire trip itinerary will be disrupted – and we are running it on a very tight schedule. Our induction meeting was supposed to take place before dinner and that's not going to happen now. Even dinner is going to be problematic at this late hour.

This time it's my turn to go into the terminal building to inquire. I breathe deeply and frame the question deferentially, careful not to slip into sarcasm. The woman at the airport information desk looks up dully.

"The Miami flight? All I know is what you know. It's on the screen behind me."

"With respect, according to the screen, the flight has been en route to Havana for three hours and the journey takes less than an hour."

She shrugs and her eyes glaze over. Cuban bureaucrats, especially the women, seem to have perfected this technique. They don't even glance away or pretend to be busy, they stare right at you, dully, making it clear that they have zero interest in your problem. As there's no point in pursuing the matter, I turn to survey the uniformly grey arrivals lounge of Terminal 2. I have spent a lot of time here waiting for groups to land from Miami. It's functional, a place of transit, uncomplicated by shops and restaurants. A few souvenirs are on sale at a couple of stands and the solitary coffee bar is often empty, as it is now at this late hour. No flights are leaving over the next few hours, so the check-in desks in the adjacent arrivals section are deserted too.

A trickle of passengers is filtering through into the lounge from customs control. They step bleary-eyed into the fluorescent gleam, bewildered by the sudden expanse around them with no further bureaucratic hurdles to negotiate. They're my group! Over the past couple of years I have acquired the ability to distinguish tour participants from the general pageant of passengers as they emerge into the arrivals hall. Rarely do I make a mistake, although the Cuban tour guides are always more accurate; some have been doing the job so long that they never err. I step forward to a red-headed woman.

"Are you with Global Exchange, by any chance?"

The question takes a second or two to register, and then she smiles with relief. I shake her hand and introduce myself as the tour leader.

"I'm Helen," she replies, "I'm one of the college professors accompanying the group. Pleased to meet you Karen."

She introduces me to her colleagues, Sandra and Joy.

Right now we are only names, but I already know that the events, and the challenges, of the next two weeks will give us plenty of opportunities to get the measure of each other. This is the way it always starts out, with handshakes and polite introductions. Protocol prevails. By the end of the trip there'll be hugs and often tears too. For many, this is a dream come true. They've saved for months, maybe even a year or two, to make it this far and now, finally, they're here. A tour in Cuba often opens people up to a range of emotions, particularly if they have come as an expression of solidarity, as this group has. They have a large shipment of educational material, mostly books, crayons and pencils, coming in with them which they plan to donate to a primary school in the east of the country.

Just then Diana approaches and I introduce her to Helen. A few more tour participants trickle through customs and we greet them. Soon all twenty-two are gathered around and, mercifully, everyone has reconnected with their luggage, and the donations too are intact. We file out of the arrivals area into the thick humid night air to the accompaniment of suitcase wheels rumbling noisily over the walkway leading to the coach park. Juancito has woken and is opening the luggage compartment in readiness for the group. It's almost midnight. Diana whispers that she phoned the hotel earlier to arrange for a snack to be prepared for supper because the kitchen staff leaves at 10.30. It's unlikely that anyone will complain about not getting a proper dinner since the majority is college students and they look too tired to make a fuss.

Collecting a group at the airport is perhaps the most stressful part of a tour because of the likelihood that something will go wrong. Flights arrive late, passengers are often highly stressed, luggage goes missing and bureaucracy at the airport can be tricky. This group is travelling with *Amistur*, the state tour company responsible for solidarity trips, so there is a greater chance that airport bureaucrats will show flexibility, or go the extra mile to help resolve any difficulties. But it's not guaranteed. A lost suitcase or a missing visa can delay the entire group for an hour or more. Tonight's start is shaky, but at least everything and everybody has arrived safely. We've been held up for over three hours this evening so it's a relief to be on the bus to the hotel.

This group's itinerary is fairly standard for the first few days. They go on a sightseeing tour of Havana, by bus – or by bike, if they wish – to the scale model of the city, then on a guided walking tour of Old Havana, and after that comes a visit to La Cabaña fortress, where they see the nightly ritual of the canon being fired, just as it was in colonial times. On Day 3 we leave Havana and head east, through Santa Clara, and south to Trinidad, where we will spend two nights.

When we get to Trinidad there is a problem with the accommodation, a potentially serious problem. There aren't enough free rooms in our hotel. We discover this on our arrival at around 8.30 in the evening. This is one of the worst organisational predicaments we can find ourselves in. While the group sits on the coach, out of earshot, Diana, the receptionist and I do the maths and juggle names around until we find beds for everyone ... except ourselves. They can accommodate us on the second night of our stay, but not that evening. When the last of the group has vanished into the lift with their suitcases, we ask the receptionist to call nearby hotels in an effort to find accommodation. Half a dozen phone calls later and we have to accept that everywhere is fully booked for tonight. There's one other solution, I say to Diana: we must try the local Bed & Breakfast options, *casas particulares*. She reminds me that neither she nor Juancito is allowed to stay in a privately run guesthouse ... even if they could afford it. I offer to pay, but she won't allow it.

"We have no choice at this point. What's the alternative? Sleeping on the coach?"

"Yes, on the coach. Remember that I'm an employee of the state and I'm here on an assignment. I'll lose my job, Karen, if they find out I've been sleeping in a private guesthouse."

We board the coach and tell Juancito that he may not have a bed that night. He too won't consider the option of a guesthouse, even though he has to drive the following day. It's too risky.

"I'm not going to jeopardise my job by renting a guesthouse room. That's that."

He is going to sleep on the coach whatever happens, and we are welcome to join him. It won't be the first time this has happened.

I set off with Diana in search of a bed. We call at five random B & Bs to inquire about a room and at each one we are told that they cannot rent to Cubans. Diana looks humiliated and angry, while I plead with them to reconsider. In the last house, two elderly ladies want to help – they have spare rooms – but they look frightened.

"Our licence to rent will be withdrawn if we are caught giving lodgings to her. It's our only source of income. What can we do? Perhaps we could contact the authorities and clear it with them first."

By now it is almost 11.00 pm.

Diana urges me not to insist any longer. She's going to join Juancito, so I walk with her to the porch. "Look at their faces," she says, referring to the nervous B & B owners.

"Is this a normal society? These old women are desperate to help yet they're too terrified to do the right thing. Is it right that two professionals have to sleep on the floor of a coach in the course of their duties because it is forbidden for them to rent a room in a guesthouse? This is bureaucracy gone mad. Where's the democracy in this mess?" she hisses.

Just then one of the old ladies emerges to suggest that I rent the twin-bedded room and my name alone appears in their register. Officially, Diana never stayed here. As an added precaution they ask Diana to leave at dawn, and to skip having breakfast on the premises.

The following day, Juancito is hollow-eyed but at least he has managed to shave and change clothes in the men's toilets at the hotel. The tour participants have no idea that he had to sleep on the coach, or that there was any problem at all last night. They're really excited about spending the day on the Ancón beach ... their first taste of the Caribbean.

After leaving Trinidad, we continue eastward, stopping in Camagüey and Las Tunas and following the road to Bayamo, the last town before we tackle the Sierra Maesta. The students are in their late teens and early twenties so they pass the hours on the road playing games and listening to music on their personal stereos. Group dynamics are healthy, buoyant even; there are no personality clashes and enthusiasm for the trip seems to grow with each passing day. This is perhaps one of the most energetic and generally positive tours I've been on. The highlight of this particular itinerary, *In the Footsteps of Che*, is an excursion to the mountains of the Sierra Maestra, where Fidel Castro and Che Guevara established their headquarters during the three-year battle they led against the Batista dictatorship in the late 1950s.

By the time we arrive in Bayamo, which is about 750 kilometres from Havana, we've been on the road for almost a week. Many of the students are nursing hangovers as they've been partying night after night in all the towns we've visited. Since alcohol in Cuban bars is not as cheap as they had been hoping for, the parties have largely taken place in their hotel rooms with $5.00 bottles of Havana Club rum mixed with litres of *Tropicola*. Not exactly a Cuba Libre, but it does the job as far as the students are concerned. Helen whispers to me that she's much happier this way, with them being in their rooms, particularly the girls, given the amount of attention they are receiving from the Cuban male population. I reassure her that there are very strict rules about Cubans not entering a hotel room. The girls might try to outfox security on the hotel doors but Cubans won't risk it because they know that trespassing, entering a hotel room in a dollar-paying establishment, is taken very seriously.

We stop at the ICAP offices to collect the representative for the area, Elizardo Rodríguez, who will join us for the next four days. He's a somewhat portly figure, a kind of tropical Santa Claus, without the red and white gear. When he climbs on the coach, I formally introduce him to the group of three college lecturers before he addresses the group. Protocol is important with college (and professional) groups because there is a question of rank involved. There are now three of us, plus the college professors, in a position of authority. I've seen this go badly wrong before, in a clash of male egos, so I'm relieved that Diana is our guide. My experience this far in tourism suggests that women are more relaxed about hierarchies. Having established who is who I take the microphone and turn to the group of weary moon-faced students. The volume is too high and they snap to attention immediately. Once I've adjusted the sound, I tell them that we have the honour of Elizardo's company for our visit to the Sierra Maestra and that he would like to say a few words to them. I hand him the microphone, he nods to our driver, who starts the engine and pulls out onto the highway leading northward ... and eventually upward.

Elizardo starts with an explanation of ICAP's role in Cuba and its structure throughout the island. There are offices and representatives in each of the fourteen provinces. When *Amistur* – the ICAP travel agency – sends a bus to the province the local representative generally spends some time with the group, accompanying them on visits to hospitals, doctors' surgeries, schools and whatever community projects we shall visit. Very often the most educational aspect is the informal side of things, often over dinner, when the ICAP representative engages in discussion and clarification of issues raised and address questions that tour participants put to them.

Elizardo is typical of *orientales* in his ebullience and wholehearted enjoyment of the time he spends with groups. Unlike his colleagues in Havana, he has fewer opportunities to interact with foreigners and practice his English, which he delights in. He's busy on the microphone now, answering a question about the "ration booklets," the supply of subsidised basics which all Cubans resident on the island have the right to. He digs his own out from the back pocket of his jeans; it's a tattered and dog-eared passport-sized booklet which he passes around for the students to see for themselves. Rice, black beans, oil, coffee, potatoes, laundry soap and milk feature on it. He has two children under the age of seven so he has the right to a litre of milk per child per day. Prices are minimal, at only a few cents for rice and for a litre of milk. Everyone seems impressed ... until they inquire about the average monthly salary.

"Between 15 and 20 dollars per month."

"A *month*?"

There are gasps all round, looks of incomprehension.

Jenny takes her headphones off ... for the first time this week.

"What's going on?"

"Even professionals, like doctors and teachers?"

Elizardo has undoubtedly been in this situation many times before with tour groups, but he still looks uncomfortable. He gathers himself and embarks on an explanation.

"Cuba is a poor country located in the developing world. We cannot allow ourselves the luxury of bestowing lavish salaries on certain individuals, no matter how important their profession is to us, leaving others to earn a pittance. At least this way, it's fair. All of us have to struggle to make ends meet and the burden is shared. This is the only way forward under socialism."

I notice after this that the students pay very careful attention to prices in the shops. A pair of jeans costs 27.00 USD, a deodorant 1.50 USD, and shampoo 2.25 USD. The maths are beyond them; the household budget beyond any of us.

"All these items, Elizardo stresses, are available in local currency, in pesos. People buy what they need with their salary in peso outlets."

Diana smirks. She knows this isn't the real picture. Many products are just not available in these peso stores, and, if they are, the quality is abysmal. Yet the myth of how Cuba provides for all its citizens has to be upheld. It occurs to me that if only party hacks and apologists would admit to the shortcomings of the system their words might carry greater credibility.

"Can we visit one? A peso store? Can we have a look at what they sell?"

Our ICAP representative looks even more uncomfortable so I step in.

"There are plenty in Havana. When we get there, if you are still interested, I'd be happy to take you."

Elizardo swiftly guides the discussion on to safer territory, to the past.

"Where we are going today is historic, for it was here, in the heart of the Sierra Maestra mountains, that President Fidel Castro, his brother Raúl, Che Guevara and their band of guerrilla fighters waged the battle that brought down the dictatorship of Fulgencio Batista and ushered in the Revolution. That was back in 1959. It took them three years to succeed and we are going to take this opportunity to retrace their steps. We'll go into the mountains and see their headquarters for ourselves."

Just then our driver, Juancito, pulls to a stop and calls Elizardo over to him. They confer for a minute or so. From the concerned looks on their faces it is apparent that something is wrong. They beckon to me and Diana. It turns out that our coach is an older model and Juancito is doubtful about its ability to climb the hills that lie between us and our hotel in the tiny mountain village of Santo Domingo. We stop at the base of the steepest hill I have ever seen. Someone a few seats behind me remarks that the gradient would be illegal in the United States.

"What we really need is a fifth gear for the ascent and hydraulic brakes for the descent. Our coach has neither," whispers Juancito.

"So what do you recommend?"

He looks up at me apologetically.

"Walking."

We agree to let Juancito drive on at his own pace and for us to follow on foot. It will take a couple of hours longer, but it's safe. The students are elated at the prospect of getting out of their seats and eagerly rush towards the exit.

All twenty-five of us set off, walking on occasions at an angle of what must be about 65º to the perpendicular tilt of the road. The landscape is undoubtedly the most magnificent that I've seen so far in Cuba. Lush vegetation springs from sheer drops, and abrupt upward sweeps arrest the gaze and guide it skyward into the clouds. The sky is shrunk, framed by verdant peaks. I too am shrunk, made delightfully small, humbled by the power of these mountains. I remind myself that I am in the east of Cuba, somewhere between the Caribbean and the Gulf of Mexico, surrounded by landscape which has not changed in millennia. All of us are quiet now, content to pay homage to the moment, knowing that it will never come again. Around us there is birdsong, insistent calls produced by exotic creatures I cannot see and cannot name.

An ugly clattering, suggestive of metal colliding with concrete, intrudes on my reverie. It is getting louder, faster, and it's coming toward us. From around the bend – at speed – comes a *chivichana,* a guider, steered by an elderly *campesino*, his face frozen into a grimace. G-force, or perhaps the immensity of effort required to keep his vehicle under control at such speed? It's not clear. Both hands are on the reins, guiding his "vehicle" to the side of the road; legs outstretched, heels slammed against the front wheels, jamming them to a halt a few metres away. Mules and home-made guiders are the most common forms of transport in the Sierra. The students are already gathering around enthusiastically. I stay back, content to watch and let the encounter develop under its own dynamics. A few words are exchanged in broken Spanish between the wizened, bright-eyed sprightly driver and his admirers.

"*Qué lindo*. What a beautiful guider. Did you make it yourself? What speed do you go? Is it dangerous?"

And then, inevitably: "Would you mind if we take a few photos?

Photos taken, the students give the old man the thumbs up and he manoeuvres his *chivichana* into position to continue its downward journey. Just as he is about to lift his heel-brake from the front wheels one of the group calls out to him: "*Señor! Señor! Por favor."*

We turn our heads to see Jeremy, one of the quieter boys, hoist a bottle of Havana Club rum on high:

"*Muchas gracias!*"

And then he tosses it with a long slow motion to the old man who catches the bottle in a single deft sweep of the hand. Only a talented baseball player would have been capable of such elegance, and everybody applauds. Then he is gone in a flash, followed by a rapidly retreating commotion that can be heard echoing through the mountains for a minute or two after we have lost sight of him. We see more *chivichanas* over the next few days; sometimes they are little more than a blur as the locals power down these slopes at breakneck speed on this most unique form of transport.

The road takes us to our hotel, the Villa Santo Domingo, where we are going to spend the next three nights. Diana and Elizardo announce to the group that Fidel sometimes comes to stay here when he wants to reconnect with nature and with his youthful past. They know that everyone would love the honour of staying in "his" room and sleeping in "his" bed, so to be fair a raffle is going to be held. All the keys are placed in a cowboy-style straw hat, typical of the ones worn by men on horseback in these parts, and the process of selection begins. When everyone has selected a key Elizardo declares the winner. Helen and Joy, history and politics respectively, both screech with delight. They have drawn the key to cabin Number 6, Fidel's room. There is a certain justice in such a chance win for these self-effacing teachers, the students generously applaud and congratulate each of them in turn. Later, I ask Elizardo if he manipulated the raffle, but he denies it.

"How could I? You saw what went on."

The students go off to their rooms, which are in a scattering of wooden cabins spreading into the surrounding glades beside the river that flows down from the mountains. Diana invites me to go for a stroll with her, to get a measure of the place, as this is her first trip as a tour guide to the area. She tells me that when she was a university student she climbed the highest peak in the Sierra Maestra, the Pico Turquino, as all young people are encouraged to do in Cuba. It is almost 3,000 metres high, and the heat, humidity and dense forestation mean that many don't make it to the summit. Members of the Young Communist League (UJC) regard the ascent as a sort of pilgrimage, undertaken in homage to the guerrilla fighters who hid out here during their struggle against Batista. We are not going to the Pico Turquino tomorrow. Instead, we are hoping to make it to the Rebel Headquarters (*Comandancia de la Plata*), which stands about 2,000 metres above sea level.

Our stroll is cut short when three geese down by the river suddenly resent our presence and launch a ferocious attack, honking, flapping their wings and pursuing us back up the path to the hotel reception. Diana goes off to our room while I take advantage of the lull to call home. Incredibly, the line is working and Alexis picks up the phone. He hasn't been home for the past few evenings and we need to talk. Tomorrow evening he takes a flight to Madrid and won't be returning to Cuba. He is the personal physician of a leading classical composer, and will be accompanying his patient on a trip to Spain. This is his chance, our chance, to finally begin the life that we have been planning for three years.

"So where have you been the past few nights? I've called but you weren't home." Tension edges my voice.

Alexis replies that he wanted to spend time with his family, reminding me that he doesn't know when, if ever, he'll see them again. Now the tension edges his tone. I am silent, conscious of the potential for this conversation to turn into another row.

"I'll miss you," he says.

"Well, you know the plan. Get yourself sorted out and send word when you want me to join you. But don't leave it too long."

"I won't. I can't be on my own there. I've never been out of Cuba before and now I'm facing a lifetime away from the only place I've ever known. They'll never let me come back."

His voice is crumpled, nervous. I soften my tone.

"Just keep in mind all the reasons why you're leaving. Write them down on a piece of paper, if it helps. Read them when you get there."

Alexis replies but I can't make out what he's saying. The line or the emotion is cracking and fuzzing his voice. I tell him to call me when he reaches Madrid and end by saying how much I love him, but there is no reply, just silence. It's not clear how much he has heard of my last couple of sentences.

Conspiracy has become the basis of our relationship. We've been conspiring ever since Alexis and his team lost their bonuses. An unannounced inspection of the operating theatre found breaches of protocol, and these were reported to management. Penalties were applied and, for the second time in two years, the surgeons and nurses lost an opportunity to receive a dollar bonus. It was the last straw as far as Alexis was concerned. He was angry and humiliated. There and then he swore that he would join the handful of his colleagues who have "defected" to Spain or Latin America over the past couple of years. The opportunity to do so has finally arisen.

Breakfast is early, at 6 am. While we are still eating two lorries arrive and begin revving their engines in the car park. Elizardo announces that they are Soviet lorries with hydraulic brakes and five gears. The word "Soviet" raises a few eyebrows and the students look impressed. I am not sure what hydraulic brakes means in mechanical terms but it sounds reassuring. The students file out into the car park and locals hoist them up - about two metres - onto the back of the lorries. A pair of park rangers, our guides for the day, join us and immediately strike up conversations in laudable English with Helen, Joy and Sandra. Once everybody is aboard, we are advised to sit down, hold on tight and enjoy the ride into the heart of the Sierra Maestra National Park.

Both engines roar and growl as the vehicles swing round, ponderously, to face the challenge: a terrifyingly steep ascent that at times makes us feel as if we are about to free fall off the back of the lorry. My un-mechanical mind cannot grasp how these vehicles resist the pull of gravity, and cling to a surface that appears to be at a right angle to the tyres. Ivan, one of the park rangers, says that the road is a feat of civil engineering, specially designed with ridges that help the rubber adhere to the concrete. Each time we negotiate one of the hairpin bends I smell burning rubber and I can only hope – selfishly – that it is coming from the other vehicle. Diana jokes with the students about the danger, but some of the group still looks tense.

Just as I'm beginning to personify the engines, empathising with their pitiful hissing and wheezing, we reach the end of our ascent on a road which is, in all likelihood, the steepest in the world. It's taken us just over half an hour to get here but it feels like much longer. For the rest of the journey we shall follow a rocky path on foot. There is the option of mules, but nobody is brave or foolish enough to accept. We thank our drivers and leave them to wait for us in their trucks. My descent, I vow, will be on foot, and I suspect that many of the others will be joining me.

With the element of danger gone, the group sets off, relaxed now and joking about their fears on the trucks. The park rangers are pleasant and affable; they make the ascent chatting amiably with the group, indulging our interest in the beauty and historicity of our surroundings. I endeavour to listen in whilst hopping over stones and avoiding mud on our path. Ivan and his colleague Yosmel know a great deal about the flora around us, and they are enthusiastic about sharing their knowledge with whoever happens to be closest.

Yosmel tells me that he has a wife and three small children in the village of Santo Domingo. He studied zoology in the University of Santiago and taught himself English – more or less – so that he could find a decent job in tourism. His father makes a living from a coffee plantation, so being a park ranger and tour guide is, he acknowledges, quite a break in the family tradition. The mention of coffee reminds me that the Sierra Maestra is reputed to be the best coffee-growing region in the country. I glance behind me, checking to make sure that Elizardo is nowhere near.

"Can I buy some from him, from your father?"

Yosmel looks hesitant. I've been too direct. So I rephrase the question.

"If there is any chance of anyone in the village selling us some coffee beans, around twenty kilos, we'd be very grateful."

He nods and replies that he'll do what he can. Black market deals carry sanctions. Coffee producers have to sell to the state at fixed prices, not on the free market. Still, the invitation to sell is out there and I'm hopeful.

After almost two hours, we pause at Alto del Naranjo, where a *campesino* serves us cups of locally grown and roasted coffee. The group gathers in small clusters on the front porch of the homestead, from where we can see the Pico Turquino rising above the rest of the Sierra Maestra mountain range. The view is spectacular and the air is probably crisper up here than anywhere else in Cuba; yet we feel the heat of the sun growing with each passing hour, even though it is only early February. I'm grateful that lush vegetation has shaded us this far. The rocky path and slippery conditions have made the ascent much harder than I had anticipated and I see that Sandra, who is probably in her late fifties, is beginning to flag. When Yosmel mentions that the second leg of the trek is perhaps even more demanding, she decides that she will remain here at Alto del Naranjo and wait for us to return.

The students are undeterred by the challenge, and eagerly race after Yosvel, who is taking up the lead. I wonder how well they would fare if the temperature rose another ten degrees, as it could in mid-summer. I wonder how I would fare.

Before joining them I head off in the direction of the toilet. It is in a tiny wooden hut at the end of a narrow path, about fifty metres away from the homestead. Half way along the path the stench hits me; a few metres further and I hear the thick and heavy drone of flies. I've been in Cuba long enough to brave this, I tell myself, so I pull out a tissue, cover my face, and advance. The door of the hut swings open easily and it takes my eyes a few moments to adjust to the darkness within. It is a typical rustic construction consisting of two wooden planks, which serve as the seat, set parallel to each other over a pit. I would have to manoeuvre myself onto the planks and lever my rear over the space between them in a kind of "bombs away" exercise. It takes me one second to realise that a false move on my part, a slip, would see me plummet into the pit below, because the planks are not properly secured. Besides, I see that not all the previous users have been accurate in their manoeuvres. Flies are crawling over pieces of excrement stuck to the planks. I retch and flee into the forest in search of a bush, disregarding all my previous concerns as to whether my rear end would catch the eye of one of the local *campesinos*.

An hour later and I am standing with some of the students outside Fidel's wooden cabin at the Rebel Headquarters. It's in better condition than some of the others in the glade but it is still very much a makeshift affair. As I peer in I try to imagine him stooping to accommodate all 6' 3" of his frame under this palm leaf roof and how it must have been when crucial decisions were taken here, in the very nerve centre of a power struggle that changed the history of this country and, arguably, this part of the world, forever. A bullet hole in the side of the fridge is the only sign of the dangerous moments that these walls have witnessed. In the background there is birdsong and the trickle of a brook below where, Yosmel tells us, Fidel used to bathe.

Further up the hill is Che Guevara's cabin, and beyond that is the very first base of Radio Rebelde, set up to publicise the struggle in Cuba and abroad. Elizardo explains that the first transmissions reached far off parts of Latin America, but not Havana or the rest of the island. Getting the frequency and power of the signal right took a few weeks, but when they did, Radio Rebelde became a crucial part of the propaganda war against Batista. I marvel at how, in the midst of this mountain wilderness, with minimal resources, these men waged a successful military offensive and a propaganda war. Momentarily, I'm ashamed that I was incapable of shuffling off my attachment to the comforts of civilisation, even for the few minutes it takes to use a rustic toilet.

Our descent is as taxing, both physically and mentally, as I had feared. Almost every foothold has to be carefully chosen. Some of the group slips in the mud, but nobody twists an ankle. When we finally reach the waiting Soviet trucks, only a handful of the students are brave enough to climb back up on to them. The three lecturers, who are too weary to worry about the danger, join them. Once they have departed, the rest of us put our feet forward and lean back into the perpendicular. That's the position we maintain to resist the pull of gravity for the next hour and a half on our descent. So steep is it that Fidel Castro once remarked that this road resembled more of a vertical landing strip than a highway. With the constant forward pressure jamming my toe nails tightly up against the front of my trainers, I arrive limping at Villa Santo Domingo, nursing badly bruised and blistered toes, and probably the beginnings of ingrown toenails. One of the students turns to me grinning.

"It's all part of the adventure."

I smile, recalling that I'd used the same line the previous afternoon when the geese launched their attack on Diana and me.

That evening, over dinner, Elizardo announces that he has arranged for the Rebel Quintet to give a performance tonight at the hotel. These musicians entertained Fidel's men up in the mountains during the campaign against Batista and fifty years later are still performing. On hearing the announcement, Helen whispers to me: "If this trip gets any better, I won't be able to take it. I'll just die."

As I make my way back along the path to my cabin after dinner, a woman with a toddler approaches and asks if I'm the tour leader. She lives locally and she'd like to know whether some of the girls would be interested in having a manicure. Cuban women are meticulous about caring for their nails, so it's not entirely surprising that even in very remote areas such as this, there are manicurists. Her name, it turns out, is Usnavy, pronounced *Oosnaavvy*. It takes a minute or two for this bizarre name to register. She's one of a number of women in the east of Cuba who have been named after the US navy base at Guantánamo. Some Cubans liked the sound so much that they have named their daughters after the installation. Interestingly, the authorities never objected when parents came to register their child.

Usnavy whispers that she's not allowed to engage in private business on hotel property so any work she does will have to be discreet, in her own home. The students may never have such an opportunity again, the opportunity to see what life is like inside one of the local *bohio* cabins, so I tell her that I'll talk to the girls about it.

The following evening Usnavy is waiting for me by the hotel entrance. She looks anxious when she sees that seven of the girls – and one of the boys - are following me.

"You didn't tell Elizardo that you were coming here, did you?"

"Of course not. I wouldn't want to cause problems."

The tension fades somewhat from her features.

"Let's go quickly then."

The students are more enthusiastic about visiting the manicurist's home than having their nails beautified, but I don't tell her that. Instead I whisper that it'll be okay. Helen is the only lecturer who wants to come with us. As we walk up the road away from the Villa Santo Domingo, she confesses that she feels like a voyeur.

Usnavy leads us along a short track that veers off the road and ends at her front porch. She quickly urges all of us to step inside, ostensibly because the mosquitoes are out, in reality it's because she doesn't want the neighbourhood association (CDR) to know we are here. We crowd inside but the palm-leaf roof is so low that some of the students have to stoop. In these diminutive surroundings they look taller than they really are. For most of us there's nowhere to sit. A solitary electric bulb hangs from the central wooden beam, casting a dim and fuzzy mustard light across the only furniture in the room, a Formica-top table and four wooden chairs. The floor is red earth, hardened and flattened over time. From where I stand I can see the kitchen and the bedroom, the only other rooms in the *bohio*. There is a narrow track leading away from the back yard, threading its way into the gloom beyond, where I presume the latrine is located. I hope the students have had the foresight to use the toilet in the hotel.

It's too cramped for all of us to remain for long so I organise the group on an appointment basis. Each manicure takes half an hour and those at the end of the list wander back to the hotel. Fearful of losing their custom, Usnavy is reluctant to let them go. I point out that it's unfair to make them stand, or sit around for hours waiting for a manicure. Now that they've seen the poverty in which her family lives, she says looking crushed, they may not want to come back. I shrug my shoulders, thinking that whatever they decide to do, she will have made more money in these few hours than she has ever made at any other time in her life ... and she's only charging one dollar per person.

Over the next couple of manicures, I learn that Usnavy has four children, and a fifth is on its way, although it doesn't show yet. She is slender with soft melancholic features that suggest she might be of indigenous descent. If any trace of the pre-Columbian Taino and Siboney peoples wiped out by the Spaniards centuries ago is to be found in the modern day Cuban population, it is likely to be in these mountainous regions. When I ask if she wants more children, Usnavy responds with an indifferent shrug of the shoulders.

"You could choose. Would you consider using a contraceptive? "

Her husband won't agree to it but she doesn't elaborate on his reasons. There's no need to for I can guess that the test of virility in these parts lies in the number of children a man fathers. Such considerations often outweigh any concerns for the woman's health or the couple's ability to provide for a growing family.

As I'm leaving, Usnavy's husband arrives with their four children; all of them appear to be under six. Contrary to what I had imagined, he's not a pot-bellied drunkard and he doesn't swagger. In fact, he's softly spoken, slightly built and young, no more than twenty-five. At least on the surface, they would seem to be the ideal couple. I've been arrogant to presume to know what goes on between these walls. Chastened, I walk back down the hill to the Villa Santo Domingo alone.

As I enter the parking area of the hotel a figure moves in the shadows, beckoning me.

"*Señora*, the coffee."

I look across to see two men are standing in the corner of the car park, by our coach. When I come closer I notice two large sacks resting against a nearby tree. I peer inside one of them and sniff; there's no hint that the contents are coffee.

"Coffee only smells good when it's roasted," one of them whispers.

Their asking price is ridiculously low for 20 kilos and I add an extra ten dollars by way of thanks for their taking the risk. The men are overjoyed, but so am I because I've just acquired six months' supply of the very best coffee on the island, and from the same area where Fidel obtains his supply. Getting it back to Havana shouldn't be a problem because the police don't search tourist buses.

Four days later and we are back in Havana unloading the suitcases from the coach for the very last time. The girls still sport expertly manicured nails as they queue at the check-in desk for the Miami flight in Terminal 2. Those nails, Usnavy's imprint on their lives, will soon be in a metropolis that might as well be a million miles away from her tiny *bohio* home in the Sierra Maestra Mountains. For my part, although I'm tired, I'm sad to see them leave. This tour group has been particularly appreciative, and I'm confident they won't easily forget her, or the experiences they have had on this trip.

Diana and I leave Terminal 2 after the last of the group file through immigration control into the departure lounge. Juancito is waiting for us on the coach and as soon as we board he pulls out. In about ten minutes Diana will get off at a crossroads and return home to await word of her next assignment. After such an intense experience, working together night and day for over two weeks, the separation is always an anti-climax. I've grown fond of Diana and I don't know if or when I'll see her, or Juancito, our driver, again. All three of us will be absorbed back into the day-to-day social fabric of a society we market again and again to the tour groups we work with. The longer I live here the greater the discrepancy appears to be between the Cuba that I present to visitors and the reality of the country as I experience it.

Each time we attend a social event, a street party held by the neighbours belonging to a local CDR in honour of a visiting group, I'm aware that these people who are joking and dancing with American tourists may be the ones who spitefully inform on their neighbours for selling takeaway dishes from their home without a license, for renting rooms illegally to foreigners, or for building a boat on which to flee the island. In Santiago, the night after one such street party, a ten-year-old girl knocks at the door of the house where I'm lodging. She's going from house to house with a list the CDR has given her, and she's ticking off the names on it. It's an important day. It's 26 July, the anniversary of the Moncada Rebellion, and Fidel is giving a speech in the city this evening to commemorate the occasion. Neither I nor the family I'm staying with is attending. It's too hot and, besides, we are well aware that the speech could continue for hours. The list, the child explains, is so that the CDR has a record of who in the area is not attending the speech. My friend doesn't rise from her armchair. She rolls her eyes.

"But we're watching it on TV, doesn't that count? Besides, I've got a baby and have to look after her."

The girl seems satisfied with the explanation, but she ticks a box on her list anyway and leaves.

The contradictions of my work haunt me. Doctors who give our groups presentations on the benefits of *Health for All* under socialism may also be the same ones who accept gifts, even is if it is just a suckling pig or a few gallons of petrol, in gratitude for ensuring that grandma's hip replacement proceeds without her joining a long waiting list. Teachers who extol the virtues of free universal education for the population fail to mention that morale is so low that recruitment drives for teaching professionals are floundering. Having decided (in 2000) to cap primary school pupil numbers per class at twenty in a bid to improve the quality of education, the government was faced with a shortage of teachers. Recruitment campaigns had limited success so, to cope with the extra demand, high-school graduates and first-year university students are being encouraged onto fast-track diplomas that see them take on hefty teaching timetables and even managerial responsibilities while they are still in their late teens.[v] People earn salaries in Cuban pesos, in a currency which excludes them from the vast majority of retail outlets, the so-called "dollar shops" which my groups presume supply the nation.

At times I feel like a fraud. But there's nothing I'm prepared to do about it. Exposing these hypocrisies to tourists is not going to make life any easier for Cuban people; nor is it going to please the tour participants. Many, but not all, arrive on the island with stars in their eyes, keen to get up close to a society that has been so ostracised by their own government. I ask myself what I would achieve by letting them in on some of the more unpalatable secrets of the

Revolution. Nothing. Life in Cuba would continue on as it did before, whereas exposure to the uglier aspects of life on the island would demoralise and disappoint. That's not what the business of tourism is about, not even educational or reality tourism.

CHAPTER 9

What Can You Do For Me?

The shop assistant is just putting the finishing touches to an exquisite work of art – her nails. She arches her back, extends both arms parallel and stretches her fingers full length to get the maximum effect. We both zoom in on her *pièce de résistance* from this new angle. She has chosen a background of iridescent blue and streaked it with delicate flashes of white. It puts me in mind of lightning as it is reflected in the waters of the Gulf of Mexico at twilight when a storm is approaching from a distant horizon. My reverie is interrupted when she hollers over to a colleague,

"Oyé, Odalys, come and see my nails. It's taken me over half an hour to finish them. It's a new colour. Marisleisy's cousin brought it from Miami."

Odalys replies crossly that she's busy doing the till.

Only when she begins to blow on her nails, fanning her fingers rapidly under her pursed lips and glancing around idly, does she become aware of my presence. I've been standing here at the counter for a full five minutes watching, fascinated as much by the nails as by her ability to remain entirely oblivious to me when I'm only a metre away. I'm her last customer today, or at least I hope to be, because if she doesn't serve me in the next thirty seconds the big hand of the clock will touch twelve and it will be five on the dot, too late to make my purchase. I'm conscious that the seconds are rushing by and that she is wholly capable of slamming down a "Closed" sign in front of me, effectively turning me away. The nail polish isn't dry yet and she's unlikely to serve me while there is a risk of damaging her artwork but I'm not leaving empty-handed. I pointedly place my purchase, a bottle of hair conditioner, on the glass counter in front of me. We both glance up at the clock. Fifteen seconds to go, she glares, but doesn't dare refuse me. With a sigh and a tut

— she's stopped blowing on her nails — the assistant picks up the bottle with the utmost care and scans it. The bar code won't read. Glancing again at her artwork, she hollers to Odalys:

"I need your help. My nails aren't dry so you'll have to punch in the bar code for me."

"No can do Norma. The figures aren't adding up at my end. Gotta finish this first."

Now I shrink under the full force of a hostile glare that is every bit as threatening as the headlights paralysing a stricken rabbit caught on a country road at night. I'm indignant, but afraid to even hope that those nails will be desecrated with a false move.

Slowly and with the greatest of care, Norma keys in the sixteen figure bar code, stopping after every second or third digit to check for damage. Surprisingly, the nails survive intact and she slides the bill across the glass counter to me, again with the greatest of care. It says 2.95. I open my purse and immediately see an opportunity for revenge. She's forced me to suffer over a single purchase so now I'm going to take reprisals. I take out two one-dollar notes and — with measured deliberation - begin to count out ninety-five in coins. Just as I'm reaching ninety, I exclaim affectedly:

"What an idiot. I've made a mistake and now I have to start all over again."

So off I go, picking out ones, fives and tens from the pile and lining them up neatly, conscious all the while of a pair of highly made-up eyes boring into me with undisguised contempt. Finally, I reach the magic number, ninety-five. I slide the pile of coins across to Norma and thank her sweetly for such patience. Then I turn to leave the deserted premises.

I'm in the shopping centre on the corner of 5ta y 42 (Fifth Avenue and 42nd Street), a characterless precinct situated on Fifth Avenue in the elegant Miramar neighbourhood. Cubans call these hard currency outlets "la shopping" (pronounced "chopping") or sometimes, the diminutive, "la shoppingcita." Some are probably unaware that in English "shopping" refers to what you buy and not where you buy it, as it is being used here, but it doesn't matter because it's been in Cuban parlance for so long now that nobody queries its etymology. Non-Cuban Spanish speakers do, however, tend to look puzzled when they hear it for the first time.

Even though customer service is undeniably poor, queues of eager shoppers regularly snake out of doorways and on to the pavement, especially at weekends. It's not unusual for bouncers to control the number entering the premises of particularly popular stores, sometimes to a degree that seems extreme. A dozen or so customers, often an apparently random number, will be counted in through the turnstile of a store and then the bouncer calls a halt; those who have got through may find themselves outnumbered by the shop assistants in attendance. Security may be so rigid that only when the last of this batch of a dozen leave, is the next dozen carefully admitted, to the annoyance of those queuing outside in the stifling heat. Tempers flare easily in these circumstances, but the last call is always with the shop management. If the crowd gets too rowdy they have been known to call the police or close the premises for the remainder of the day.

When I arrive home I'm still resentful of how I was treated in 5ta y 42. The incident was nothing out of the ordinary in terms of what is likely to happen when anyone goes shopping and yet constant exposure to such indifference is wearying. It's a sort of protracted low-intensity war waged in the arena of customer service and one more symptom of a society which I feel is losing its bearings in a haze of demoralisation. Arrogant bureaucrats and self-important shop assistants wield a degree of power that erodes patience and stamina, as well as will-power. My reserves of all three are running low.

Alexis laughs when I tell him my story about waiting for the nail polish to dry before getting served. The previous week, he says, he went to La Punta shopping complex to buy an alarm clock for his mother's birthday. He was the sole customer in the department, neither of the two assistants, who were chatting behind the counter, turned to address him. After a couple of minutes, Alexis interrupted politely to inquire about making his purchase,

"Can't you see I'm talking?" was the retort.

He waited on in silence, until the conversation had finished, in order to be served.

"What can I do Karen? If I storm out of the shop I'll have nothing for my mother at all. The nearest shop with any alarm clocks, after La Punta, is La Epoca in Central Havana. If I keep my mouth shut, I'll get what I want. That's the only smart way to go shopping in this country."

I say nothing because I've heard it all before and am drained of any sympathy I once had for him. We had a chance to lead a different kind of life and Alexis turned his back on it. That was two months ago when, after five weeks of anguished deliberation in Madrid, he packed his suitcase and boarded the return flight to Havana as part of the Cuban medical team he was assigned to. Numerous costly phone calls during those weeks, in which I pleaded with him to stay in Spain until I joined him as we had planned, led to nothing. Alexis didn't have the courage that it takes to become a deserter, as they are called in Cuba. The night he flew back I refused to open the door of our home in Jaimanitas to him.

"Outside of Cuba I was lost," he pleaded. "I think I'm institutionalised, like a prisoner. The fear of freedom was terrifying. Try to understand me."

I couldn't even try so he disappeared into the darkness, presumably to stay at his parents' house.

A few days later I gave in and opened the door but my mood has been sour since. We are right back to where we started after two and a half years of planning and scheming, only now we're directionless. The daily grind of power cuts, bureaucratic hurdles, the losing battle to get some kind of balance in my diet, endless queues and the overwhelming sense of being cut off from the outside world is making me bitter and resentful about my life in this country. My time in Cuba is running out.

The stories that I hear of unbelievable rudeness and brazen corruption harden my resolve to leave. Some shop workers, including acquaintances of mine, are relatively wealthy in comparison to other state sector workers such as journalists, doctors and scientists; they drive cars, build extensions to their homes, hire maids and own mobile phones. Their privileges, I'm told, are financed by manipulating the weights of products sold and the prices too, as well as by straightforward theft. There is a mechanism called "*la multa*", which Sonia explains to me. At first I'm puzzled because I translate the term literally as "a fine" but it's not a fine, rather it's commission on goods purchased. A percentage is added to the recommended selling price by sales staff and when the item is sold, they keep the difference. The price of the same pair of shoes or air-conditioning apparatus varies according to the amount of commission added to the original price. So it is the daring of shop workers, as opposed to the mechanism of competition, which determines prices. The entire practice is illegal but there has been very little progress in official attempts to prevent it spreading because – I'm told – government inspectors are being paid off to keep quiet.

Occasionally there is a spanner in the works, when an honest inspector arrives on the scene or there is a clampdown from above. This is what eventually happens to

La Punta department store. I am told that advance warning was received that the authorities had ordered a thoroughgoing inspection, with the aim of exposing corruption. Fraud had become so blatant and widespread that people were using the term metastasis to describe its presence in all commercial transactions at La Punta. The figures did not add up on any level and there was no backtracking, no way of covering up. On the eve of the inspection, perhaps in recognition that the situation had become unsalvageable, somebody took drastic action. Flames consumed the premises in hours and the evidence vanished, quite literally going up in smoke.

Visiting friends or tour participants often ask me how to distinguish outlets – like those in La Punta - selling in hard currency and others who deal in pesos. First I explain that there are three currencies circulating: Cuban pesos, which is how Cuban workers are paid, then there are U.S. dollars and their Cuban equivalent, the CUC (Cuban Convertible Peso), known locally as *chavitos*. All dollar shops accept both *chavitos* and American dollars, whereas peso shops will not, unless the shopper is prepared to accept their change in pesos. Then I point out that peso shops are conspicuous by their generally shabby appearance. Paint has long since peeled away from the exterior, while the interior is generally drab and gloomy, staffed by lacklustre assistants who show minimal interest in selling the few items that are scattered around dusty shelves. Peso shops sell a limited selection of what is frequently poor quality and uninspiring clothing, footwear and furniture to those who have no income but their peso wage. Merchandise sold in these shops is often cheaper than their hard currency counterparts, but the quality is frequently disappointing.

It is rare to see queues at peso outlets, unless a batch of something unusual arrives and word gets out about it. That's when security is required. One morning on Calle Monte in Central Havana I see a crowd of maybe sixty or seventy people, spilling on to the pavement outside a health food shop. Curious as to what might have attracted them, I cross the street to have a closer look. From the doorway I see that the section of the shop selling the much-sought-after item is cordoned off; the rest of the premises are bereft in comparison. A six-foot-something security guard is allowing customers through two at a time,

"Only four packets per person," he warns as they pass.

I pause, curious to see what a nation of professed meat eaters could find of interest in a health food shop marketing vegetarian products. Two women emerge, each with their quota of four packets tucked under their arms.

"What is it?"

They clasp their purchases even more tightly.

"Soya," they bark back at me.

Then I remember. Cubans blend soya -textured vegetable protein (TVP) with mince to bulk it out. At a subsidised price of only two pesos (10p) per packet, this is excellent value, considering the amount of protein contained in TVP.

For me the most dismal retail premises on the island have to be the *bodegas*, the stores which sell the produce featured on the national ration booklet, known as the *libreta*. Every Cuban family has a *libreta*, but it is probably more accurate to refer to it as an official list of produce which families are entitled to purchase at subsidised prices from specific outlets, aka the *bodegas*. Walk into a typical *bodega* – there are thousands of them dotted throughout the island – and you will see sacks of rice, black beans, sugar, salt, coffee, potatoes and litre bags of milk and soya yoghourt. Sometimes there are boxes of eggs, barrels of cooking oil, blocks of soap, tubes of toothpaste and crates of chicken pieces. As the store holder hands the items over to the customer he or she ticks the ration booklet accordingly as proof that the items have been assigned. The cost is nominal because the subsidy reduces the price far below what the same produce would fetch on the free market.

One of the problems with the *bodega* is that produce is sold as and when it becomes available and supply is erratic. The fact that an item features on the ration book list is no guarantee that it will actually end up in the household. Queues form when word spreads about deliveries of such prized items as chicken, eggs or toothpaste. After that, there is no choice but to wait for the next batch, which could take days, weeks or even longer. People who work full time run the risk of missing out. A handy solution – if there is enough spare cash – is to pay a messenger to queue for you, and buy from the family ration book. All over Cuba hundreds, maybe thousands, of people make a modest living out of working as a messenger for a dozen or so families. Messengers get to know about deliveries by remaining friendly with the store holder, who is very possibly rewarded for passing the word out to his "favourite" clients.

Everything in the ration book can be bought on the free market, but more expensively. Unsubsidised black beans, cooking oil, soap, coffee can be bought at any of the hard currency supermarkets spread throughout the country. When their ration booklet supply runs out, as it often does, few Cubans are able, or indeed willing to fork out for products which they can often acquire at what they regard as a much more reasonable rate on the black market. It's thanks to the black market that I have a supply of powdered milk. A neighbour in Jaimanitas is my supplier. The powder is poured straight into a white plastic carried bag and weighed. It has probably been pilfered from a hotel or restaurant, or else from the nearby Ñico López Communist Party training centre – after all, that's where my neighbour's contact works.

Cheese and fresh milk are luxuries in Cuba, and I get mine from the black market. Two young women arrive in Jaimanitas at dawn every Monday morning with the milk – un-pasteurised. They bring the urns in from the countryside concealed in shopping carts. While one remains out of sight, possibly in the home of a confidante, the other arrives in my living-room and hands me three litres dispatched in two *Tropicola* plastic bottles, together with a two-pound block of fresh salty cheese, not unlike feta. I pay and give her two clean Tropicola bottles for my next delivery. She leaves, looking around carefully as she steps into the sunlight. It's risky. After three months, the women do not come again. No word is heard from them and the only people to be seen out on the street early Monday mornings are a couple of police officers, standing in the shade on the corner. It is unlikely that I'll have fresh milk or cheese again for a very long time.]

The coffee I drink is also from the black market. An elderly lady called Esperanza grinds, roasts and wraps it into neat one pound packages in her kitchen. Esperanza's hands are twisted and gnarled with arthritis, and it's painful to watch as she fumbles with the newspaper, diligently creasing and folding the pages of *Granma* around the coffee, until each packet resembles a miniature mummy. This goes into my bag. Judging by the black tornado-like stain on the wall behind her cooker, Esperanza has been toasting coffee for a very long time. I ask her where she gets it from, but she's reluctant to say.

"From the east, perhaps?"

She shakes her head,

"Impossible. All the routes from that direction are covered by police. This comes from Pinar del Río. I don't know how long the supply will hold out. They're getting nervous."

The first time I met Esperanza she had a bandage wrapped around her head, going from the top of her head down under the chin, making her face look egg-shaped. It was so tight that she could hardly move her jaw, or speak clearly.]

"Me han estirado la cara," she mumbled as she weighed the coffee into one-pound packets.

They've stretched your face? Ohhhh. A face lift?

This was a revelation for me. Esperanza has had plastic surgery as part of her health care, and it cost her nothing. It's not uncommon to encounter women living in the most decrepit homes going through with a complete physical overhaul with the local cosmetic surgeon.

"We don't pay in Cuba but I rewarded the doctor in my own way," Esperanza said pointing to a large sack of coffee beans propped up in the corner of her kitchen.

The surgery was successful, but nothing could be done about the arthritis wreaking havoc with her joints, and now there is something of a mismatch. As Esperanza puts it,

"I have the face of a fifty year old and the hands of a ninety year old."

Before I leave, I ask if I can take some flowers from her jasmine bush in the front garden. It's reputed to have sedative properties. Esperanza laughs.

"Wouldn't it be easier just to stop drinking coffee?"

When I return the following week, Esperanza's niece answers the door. She's not selling any more coffee; the police have given her aunt a warning. I wonder how the old lady will survive now on her pension of just under six dollars a month.

In Jaimanitas I depend more on black market produce than when I lived in Cerro. Except for the *bodegas*, there are no shops here and certainly no supermarkets. The nearest is about a mile away from home, and is shockingly expensive because it is on the Hemingway Marina, a resort popular with yacht crews from all over the world.

A couple of roadside stands on the main street of Jaimanitas sell fresh fruit and vegetables but the choice is poor. They sell papaya, cassava, onions and white cabbage for most of the year but that is all. If my cooking was unimaginative before, now, without inspiration, it has become relentlessly dull. Occasionally, there is mango, potato, oranges and perhaps tomato; I have to travel for a couple of miles to find greater variety.

If I'm lucky and I keep my ears open I will catch one of the travelling salesmen who sometimes drive by carrying fresh produce. My most reliable supplier is a wiry old man, *Speedy González* I call him, who flies down the street on his ancient Chinese bicycle, heavily laden with spinach, lettuce, carrot, onion and radish. When I hear his voice proclaiming the sale of produce, I rush out of the front door, race across the roof patio and down the spiral staircase into the street, calling after him. If I don't catch up, it's because he has sped on, anxious in case a police patrol spots him should he linger. On dozens of occasions I return home dejected after watching the only fresh produce I have easy access to vanish around the corner in a cloud of dust. It'll be white cabbage and onion salad for lunch again. This is the aspect of life that I least like about Jaimanitas, the lack of fresh food.

Closer to the city centre are a number of farmers' markets, known locally as *el agro*, which generally have a broad selection of fruit and vegetables at reasonable – free market – prices. The best, but also the most expensive in Havana, is in Vedado, just one block east of Paseo, at the intersection between 19 and A. Diplomats and other foreign residents swell the crowd here, along with private restaurant (*paladar*) owners, and any number of mobile sales people, offering anything from garlic to ginger to plastic carrier bags to anyone who will buy. The *agro* at 19 and A is a riot of colour and sound where dozens of stallholders call out from behind their eye-boggling displays of fresh produce, some of which cannot be found anywhere else in the city.

On my first trip to the agro at 19 and A, back in the days of *Granma International,* I learned that there is a system in place for queuing that *Habaneros* are careful to respect. Once they decide what to buy, customers call out to check who is the last in line and fall in behind them, readily answering *"Yo"* when a newcomer inquires who is *"el ultimo?"* Oddly, the predictability of the queue – and there are plenty of them in Cuba - occasionally gives me a transient sense of certainty in a country where uncertainty reigns supreme in the form hurricanes, food shortages, economic crises and, of course, power cuts.

The longest queues usually form outside *mamey* (sapote) milkshake stalls, when the sapote ripens in springtime. For two or three pesos you can buy a glass of *batido de mamey* (sapote milkshake) and it is so exquisite that many in the queue will ask for two glasses, disregarding whatever concerns they may have about drinking water that has not been boiled.

During the economic crisis of the early 1990s fuel shortages often made it impossible to transport food from the countryside, so vegetables and fruit had to be grown in the city. This dealt with the problem so effectively – and was so popular – that the resulting market gardens (*organopónicos*) flourished even after the crisis passed its acute phase. Now habaneros can drop by their local market garden for salad vegetables which were only picked that morning, mud still clinging to the roots as proof of freshness.

The nearest market garden to Jaimanitas is about five kilometres away. To get there I take a collective taxi (*máquina*) and then a bus into Miramar. It's a journey that can be exhausting in the heat, so I tend to take the lazier (and riskier) option of relying on Speedy González.

In Jaimanitas itself, bread is the only foodstuff which is always fresh and in constant supply. Just after sunrise and then again in late afternoon each day, the smell of soft white rolls baking in an industrial oven wafts across the neighbourhood and in through the shutters of my living room window. The bakery is precisely fifty-five steps from my front door. I know this because on the many days when the heat and humidity are particularly punishing, I count my steps along the street and across the wasteland surrounding the bakery. Once out of the glare and into the scant shade of the overhanging corrugated iron roof I can feel the temperature relax by two or three degrees. Queuing customers press into the wall, like civilians caught in the crossfire of a military conflict. Only when customers have their quota of bread rolls, dispatched at a cost of one peso (3p) on the free market, or at one-twentieth of that price on the ration book, do they venture back out into the direct sunlight.

During the final few months of my time in Jaimanitas, and indeed in Cuba, my neighbours convince me to buy a video recorder on their behalf. They cannot buy one themselves because the authorities have prohibited the sale of VCRs to the local population. This is because the government is determined that viewers follow Fidel's latest speech, habitually broadcast live on all three channels, as opposed to whatever American action films or South American soap operas they may have in their video collection. It took me two months to buy a VCR, and entangled me in red tape all the way from the International Press Centre (CPI) on the Rampa, and along Fifth Avenue to the shop authorised to sell it.

Only resident foreigners can buy one legally, but they have to get official permission first which, for me, means a journey to the International Press Centre (CPI). I leave with my instructions. First I choose the model of VCR I want from the shop; then I ask the CPI for written authorisation authorising the shop to give me a pre invoice, a sort of rehearsal bill. A few days later I collect the authorisation and take it to the shop. I am told to return the following week to collect my Pre-Invoice. On the following Monday following I collect it, and take it to the CPI. I'm told to return on Friday for my authorisation. On Friday, I pick up the authorisation and return to the shop for the fourth time. My VCR has been sold. I'm told to return in a fortnight. They warn me that if an identical model is not available, I will have to redraft all the documentation, starting from zero because the present authorisation and Pre-Invoice will be invalid.

Fortunately, two weeks later the correct Sony model arrives, and the shop assistant is compassionate enough to phone me as soon as it is delivered. Had the model been different I suspect I would have given up. As it is, my neighbours are delighted and insist that I have a beer and stay to watch their first video tape, ironically *Die Hard II*, to celebrate the new addition to their home.

I don't have the stamina and ingenuity that Cubans have when it comes to getting what they need to improve their lives. Outfoxing the bureaucracy is a way of life for most of my friends. As for me, I tend to shun the battle and do without, because the effort that is required to live with some degree of quality has depleted my reserves. These days I'm too tired and fed up to tackle the journey to Cerro on public transport so visit to Elisa and Tatiana are rare. Cinema and theatre are almost out of the question since Alexis is either at work, with his family, or too exhausted to accompany me to the city centre in the evening. My interest in Cuban life, rather like my diet, has become so flat that, by accepting my limited routine, I have come to resemble Alexis, institutionalised. After four years of living in Jaimanitas, I know every variation in the lap of the waves that roll in from the Gulf of Mexico, every inch of these hot and dusty potholed streets, and every careworn face that passes me. Familiar and oppressive, this reality is all that I have. To broaden my vision I rely on memories of what my life was like in Ireland, in Europe, beyond the shores of this island. This world of mine is a microcosm without the macrocosm.

With each passing year in Cuba my horizons seem to have shrunk further. Perhaps the process started – although it wasn't apparent then – during my time at *Granma*, when I was adapting to the life I had chosen to lead in Havana. There was a lot to learn and the most effective way to do that was to immerse myself in the daily challenges, not cling to Ireland and the life I had led there. The first casualty was contact with old friends, which became less frequent than I would have liked, since it depended on getting access to email. For that first year those messages were like manna. I would cycle to the house of whoever was fortunate enough to be authorised to have an Outlook account, copy the emails on to a floppy and cycle home with my treasure, anxious to read every word that friends had sent me. Later, communication became slightly easier when some Havana hotels began to offer Internet to clients and the (non-Cuban) public. By then, time and distance weakened ties, friends were not only forgetting to write to me, they were also forgetting about me. Beyond shared memories, our lives had nothing in common. I felt isolated and couldn't imagine how my Irish friends and family might begin to relate to my problems, my experiences here, and the dilemma I was now facing – my departure from Cuba without Alexis.

Leaving the island is now an imperative. I know that if I don't rejoin the outside world soon then the degree of institutionalisation will intensify. Whenever I think about returning to Ireland, I feel trapped, as if I've already missed the boat, and then anxiety floods in. Belfast has changed in the six years I have been away, good friends have left the city, I have no job to return to, and my search for one will require an artful justification of the time I have spent in

Havana. I will be starting from zero. Equally daunting is the fear that so much has happened in the outside world that I won't be able to catch up. Technology, politics, the economic situation ... I'm doomed to be perennially out of touch. I know that other foreigners living in Cuba have experienced similar crises. For some, the anxiety is so intense, especially if they have lived in Cuba for a significant part of their lives, that they cannot seriously contemplate returning permanently to their home country. Others leave and, unable to cope with the vastly changed world they encounter, return to Cuba after a few months. Surprisingly, the one person who I thought would never succeed in breaking free, would never even attempt to break free, does so. After sixteen years, Liz leaves her job as head of the English department at *Granma*, leaves her husband, packs her bags and boards a flight to New York with her two daughters. The last I hear is that she's leading a stable and contented life in her home town. I'm envious.

In the end it is a phone call from the International Press Centre that forces me to decide on a date for my departure. The official wants to see a broad sample of the articles I have been writing over the past year. I panic. Only suspicion on their part as to how I am spending my time could have prompted them to approach me about this. I have missed many official press conferences over the past couple of years and my absence must have been noticed. If they discover how much time I am devoting to translations and tour guiding they could suspend my accreditation as a member of the press corps, and that would violate my visa requirements. If that were to happen my residence permit would be cancelled, and I would be given my marching orders.

Alexis turns looks shaken when I tell him about the phone call. Neither of us has fully realised how tenuous my residence on the island was. Foolishly, we had both taken it for granted and now it is under serious threat. For a moment, I feel angry at him for having returned from Spain, but I turn away, hoping that his own logic will lead him to suffer regret for the lost opportunity

The following day I trawl through the articles I have written over the previous five years and make a selection from culture, travel and economy that I hope will satisfy the official. I delay a couple of days before emailing them to him, enough time for me to check flights back to Ireland. The following day I book and pay for a single ticket on an Air France flight to Paris with a Dublin connection. I am leaving Cuba in two weeks' time.

The Press Centre writes to acknowledge receipt of the articles and that is all they say. Their response no longer matters a great deal, since I'm going anyway. Alexis is very upset by my imminent departure and swears that if he ever gets a second opportunity to travel abroad he will not return to Cuba. The second time around, he is determined to overcome his fears.

The following week a miracle occurs. He is summoned to the Deputy Minister of Culture's office, where he is informed that in July he will be returning to Madrid with the classical composer, who again requires medical treatment there. Authorisation is being sought for Alexis to accompany him, on a delegation that includes one other doctor. He is jubilant. I'm unable to summon up any enthusiasm. I have no confidence that a new phase of scheming and plotting will lead anywhere at all.

"I'll join you, I promise. We won't be separated for long."

"We'll see."

At the check-in desk of Air France in Terminal 1 of José Martí International airport, the digital display reads 60 kilos. Ironically, I am leaving with exactly the same amount of luggage that I arrived with almost six years earlier.

The glamorous mulatta looks across the desk at me. She has my passport in her right hand and begins to fan herself slowly with it.

"You exceed the weight limit."

"Can you help me?"

She glances at Alexis momentarily and then back to me again.

"Yes, I can help you. But what can you do for me?"

The suitcases are tagged and slung on to the conveyor belt, where they begin their unwieldy journey toward the concourse and to the hold of the aircraft.

I fold a $10 bill and discreetly place it between the pages of the passport, which the mulatta has returned to me. Glancing nervously from left to right, she reaches out and takes it. Her nails are striking, white lightning streaks on a background of iridescent blue. I wonder whether she too gets her supply from Marisleisy's cousin.

"Have a good trip. Come back soon."

EPILOGUE

In July 2005, three months after I left Cuba, Alexis boarded a flight in Havana for Madrid. He and another doctor were the accompanying medical team of a distinguished musician and composer on a trip to Spain. This would be his second attempt at defecting. Shortly after landing, Alexis took the metro to Puerta del Sol, right in the heart of the city, which is where we had agreed to meet. I chose to wait for him at the spot marking *Kilometre 0* – the point used to measure distances between locations in Spain – in the hope that the symbolism would augur well for us on the journey we were about to begin.

For both of us the encounter was fraught with apprehension and doubt. Alexis looked dreadful. Dark shadows had formed under his eyes and he had lost weight since I had last seen him. Just as in Seville the previous winter, he was filled with misgivings about his ability to see this through. He insisted that he wanted to leave Cuba but the anguish in his voice suggested that in all likelihood he would be in the queue again for the Havana-bound flight at the end of the month.

"It's not just me that I have to think of. There are my parents, my son, my brother who is a Major in the Ministry of the Interior, and my ex-wife too. They're all Party members... the disgrace of having a deserter in the family will hang over them for a long time to come."

"So, what do you want to do?"

"I want to stay. We've talked about this for three years now. Here I am, I've finally got this far but I need to work up the courage to take the next step."

Alexis looked lost against a background of twenty-first century high-rise department stores and banks, the roar of traffic, flashing neon signs, sharp-suited businessmen and trendy teenagers tapping manically on their mobile phones.

"The next step?"

"Yes, I have to call them, the hospital, to tell them that I'm not going back."

His voice was thick and heavy.

"Go on. Do it then."

"I can't. I'm not ready for it. I can't do it just yet. Give me some time."

This was the line that I had heard over and over again six months previously, during those tense phone calls he made from Seville. "Give me time," he pleaded. That time, his time, our time, ran out and he returned home.

"Okay, I'll give you time. But you give me your return ticket. I'm going to rip it up."

Alexis's face froze.

"That won't achieve anything; it's an e-ticket."

Evidently Alexis was still not ready to declare himself a "deserter." Possibly no other decision in his life would have such definitive consequences, and he knew it. We were trapped in limbo and, unsure what to do there, we spent the rest of the afternoon and the following day sightseeing. Enjoyment was out of the question though. Nothing seemed real except the sickening dread that hung over us. I still can't remember where we went or what we saw on those two days.

On the third morning we went on a day trip to El Escorial, a staid crisp-aired town from where successive Spanish monarchies ruled the Americas, including Cuba, is now home to wealthy chalet-owning Spaniards. The journey was wasted because neither of us could summon any enthusiasm for a tour of the monastery, which was ostensibly the reason we had gone there. We turned our back on it and walked into the centre of the town. In a small plaza Alexis stopped and took out his mobile phone.

"I'm going to make that call," he said.

He pronounced the words as though they were a death sentence.

"Is this what you want to do? Is this really what you want to do?"

"Yes."

"Okay then. Do it."

Still he hesitated.

"Give me the phone and I'll dial the number."

Impatience sharpened my tone and I regretted it. Alexis glanced over at me and then walked away toward a set of swings in the nearby children's play area. He sat down and, digging his heels into the asphalt to stabilise himself, tapped in the number for the hospital in Havana. The call lasted less than a minute. When it was over he rose and announced that he wouldn't be retuning to Cuba.

"That was the hardest decision I have ever had to take in my life. But it's done now."

The only way to go now was forward. There was no other choice. No Plan B. Within a week we had managed to rent a small - but comfortable - flat in the centre of Madrid. Almost immediately after moving in, Alexis was offered work in a semi-private Catholic church hospital just a few metro stops away as an anaesthetist, on the condition that he started legalising his papers. Incredibly, we now had somewhere to live, and an income. Finally we were beginning to build the foundations of the life we had plotted and planned from our balcony in Jaimanitas. We were establishing ourselves in Madrid with apparent ease. Now there was a hiatus, a space in which to breathe and take account of where we were. At that very moment I made a discovery which shattered my life. It happened precisely nine days after Alexis's arrival in Spain.

In that space, in those nine days, the nagging suspicion, which I had repeatedly pushed aside in order to make room for our scheming over the past few years, would no longer be ignored. The doubts would not be banished now that Alexis was out of Cuba and there was no further plotting to do. So I went to a cybercafé in a Madrid back street, sat down at a computer and opened his email. Although I'd known the password for a few years – since the time I set up the account for him in Cuba – I had never before spied on him. What I saw on the screen stunned and sickened me. There were over a dozen messages between Alexis and two other women, clearly his lovers. One was his ex-wife whom, it became apparent as I read the emails, he had never left. The other was a hospital cleaner. Incredibly, his ex-wife had just discovered the existence of the other woman, and was enraged. She had written:

"It is one thing for me to put up with Karen, but then she has her uses, another is this trollop. You'll never change, will you?"

On that afternoon I forced myself to read every email that Alexis had written to these women and their replies. I wanted to get an exact picture of the man I had been living with for four and a half years. To both of them he pledged his love, using the very same terms of affection often recited to me, and to both he made repeated promises to get them out of Cuba once I was out of the picture. The cleaner wanted to know how long that would take, and reminisced about their sultry lovemaking sessions on the afternoons when both had managed to sneak out of the hospital, regretful that they'd come to an end. The wife's messages were venomous with resentment and jealousy. She vowed that he would never get into her bed again. The least he could do, now that he was out of Cuba, was to send money to maintain her and their son.

Discovering the extent of the lies, the web of deception that had been spun around me in this relationship, choked me with fury. Others, friends and neighbours in Jaimanitas, must have known, must have been complicit. The enormity of the betrayal defied belief.

That afternoon I confronted him in the apartment we had just rented and he denied everything – until I opened my bag and took out the memory stick I had copied the messages on to.

"Do you want me to open up the emails now, so that you can deny every word, including the lines where you promise to marry one of them once I'm out of the picture? Was it all lies in Cuba? Was anything true at all?"

He had no answer for me. I slapped his face as hard as I could.

We should have separated that afternoon, but I held on for over a year. I was in denial. It was too painful to accept that the dream which had been the focus of our lives in Cuba for so long, had turned into a nightmare, and that Dr. Jekyll had unequivocally been unmasked as Mr. Hyde. It seemed like I had been on a long journey and everything I had seen on that journey, the landscape, the people, including the man who was my companion on the journey, were not who or what they appeared to be. The relationship had no future. Trust was gone but I couldn't acknowledge that then. I looked at Alexis across a chasm filled with bitterness but held on anyway.

A few months later we moved to Rome when Alexis was offered a job in a research hospital there. That was a mistake. Not even a city famed for its romance could resuscitate what was dead and rotten. It was a travesty. In less than six weeks, I packed my bags and flew back to Belfast in the company of my cat, Thelma.

Returning home after seven years was the beginning of a brighter and more stable phase of my life. I moved back into my house and redecorated every room. I interviewed successfully for three jobs, and started teaching at a university. At the same time I began to deal with the legacy of having lived outside Europe for so long: the reverse culture shock that was preventing me from feeling at home in my own culture.

As I suspected while I was living in Cuba, the society that I had been familiar with had changed vastly, and in so many ways, that I felt alienated from it. Political leaders who had been at the zenith of their power when I left in 1999 were now historical figures, new names and faces had replaced them, wars had broken out in different parts of the world, natural disasters had taken place, technology had revolutionised communication in everyday life, and music, cinema, fashion, had all moved on. There were days, particularly in Madrid, when consumerism seemed bigger, racier and more aggressive than it had been before I left for Cuba. Avoiding large supermarkets or shopping centres became a habit and I rarely bought a newspaper or watched television. Just learning how to use a mobile phone or deciding which pizza to order from a menu that seemed to blast choices at me verged on the traumatic.

To prevent overload, I shut down as much as I could. In Madrid and Rome I engaged only in a limited way with the society I was living in. Even so, it felt like permanent overexposure to a life lived at dizzying velocity. Back in Belfast, where the pace is slower, I began to feel less estranged from my surroundings. I switched on Radio 4 every morning and read *The Guardian* at weekends; even then it took almost six months before I felt I was no longer floundering when I attempted to update myself on news and current affairs. Friends' allusions to political or cultural developments continued to baffle me – but not as much - and I gained confidence socially. It was encouraging to see that my stories about life in Cuba were popular. Friends wanted to hear about *Granma*, about Liz, Pammy, Elisa, Liliana, Ramón, Tatiana, Ana, Hilario – and of course about Deisy.

"Deisy was right," said my friend Declan.

"About what?"

"About the source of your bad luck, the evil in your house."

"What do you mean?"

"Well, didn't she say that it was a couple, mixed nationality? Cuban and foreign?"

"Yes, she did. But that was three years ago."

"You rented to Duncan and Zulema. English and Cuban, right?"

"They were friends."

"Zulema wasn't a friend to you at all. She really resented you. She was jealous and often badmouthed you when out socialising. Nothing you did for them was good enough for her."

My heart sank. For years I rented my home to a woman whom I had mistakenly believed to be a friend, of sorts. That's why I had never associated Deisy's clairvoyant insights with the people who were living in my house.

All of that is past now. I have been back in Belfast for four and a half years. My home is this tiny terraced house offering a view of a slate-grey wall defaced by six-foot-high graffiti informing me that *Kevin woz here*. Nothing about me, no such bold statement, suggests that I once lived seven thousand kilometres over there, across the Atlantic in Havana, where I was privileged to share the lives of so many unique people living in unprecedented historical circumstances. I learned much about the Cuban way of life and about myself, but perhaps the real legacy of those six years was that Cuba taught me where my home was. I am Irish and I have chosen to return to these sombre streets, where I gather my coat around me in the face of the icy northern breeze, with no regrets about leaving the Caribbean sun behind.

Adiós, Cuba.

A Brief History Of The Cuban Revolution

Cuba is very much a place apart. The traveller only has to stand on any street corner in Havana and survey the scene to recognise immediately that the revolution has left its stamp on every facet of life in this society. Clusters of young children meander by dressed in their maroon and white school uniform, topped with the blue neckerchief of the Communist Pioneers. A long line of pensioners has formed at the kiosk on the corner. They buy bundles of the two daily newspapers, *Granma* and *Juventud Rebelde* (Rebel Youth), at the price of 20 cents and resell them for one peso to supplement their income. A Ministry of Sugar "Workers' Transport" bus chugs past dodging crater-size potholes. Behind it there is a prized relic, a 1950's Chevrolet collective taxi, heading out in the direction of the Latin American School of Medicine, loaded with Honduran and Peruvian students on Cuban government scholarships. A queue snakes out of the grocery store on the corner where locals have gone to collect their subsidised rations of rice, beans and sugar. Opposite there is a slogan written in letters six feet high, *Socialism or Death. Onward to Victory*. This is the only billboard in sight. Conspicuous by their absence are the multiple trappings of consumer capitalism. No neon signs, no multinational advertising or brand names. Just this simple message.

This vista is the sum of a centuries-long dialectical process of colonialism and rebellion, beginning with Christopher Columbus' invasion of the new world five hundred years ago. Shiploads of Spanish troops disembarked on the island, heralding an era of slavery, death and pillaging for Cuba. Not until 1898 were the people of Cuba able to break free from Spanish domination. At that point, just when the Cubans were about to win their freedom, the Spanish ceded control of their colony to the U.S. Finally, four years later, Cuba gained formal independence from the United States, but only formal. The reality was that Washington agreed to withdraw its troops from the island on the condition that it retained the right to intervene in Cuban affairs when the U.S. deemed necessary (according to the Platt Amendment). Guantanamo Military Base in the east of Cuba harks back to that era. It is the continuing legacy of U.S. presence on the island, but so too is the fierce pride that ordinary Cubans take in being a free nation.

When Fidel Castro and other rebel leaders plotted the downfall of the oppressive regime of Fulgencio Batista in the early 1950s, freedom and democracy were their slogans. General strikes, bomb attacks and shootings were already ongoing in the principal cities of the island when Castro led around 160 men in an assault on the Moncada Barracks in Santiago de Cuba on 26th July, 1953. The barracks were not captured but the mood of rebellion throughout the island was heightened by the audacity of the attack. The mood, however, turned acrimonious when many of the rebels were captured and brutally tortured. Fidel Castro and his brother Raúl were among those who survived detention and were brought to trial. It was then that Castro, a young lawyer, defended himself in court, making his famous four-hour-long *History will Absolve me* speech. Neither his eloquence nor his argument were, however, enough to keep him out of jail. Both brothers were sentenced to long terms in the Modelo Prison on the Isle of Youth. Nevertheless, two years later, following widespread civil unrest, amnesties were negotiated and the Castro brothers, along with other rebels, were released to go into exile in Mexico.

Their determination to overthrow Batista remained stead forth throughout their captivity and their enforced absence from the island. On 25th November 1956, the brothers set sail in a yacht, *Granma*, from the coast of Mexico for Cuba. Eighty-two men, including the Argentine doctor, Che Guevara, were aboard the yacht. "We will be free or we will be martyrs," said Fidel Castro at the time.

Freedom came at a very high price. The yacht arrived in the Oriente province in the east of Cuba after a week at sea. As the men waded ashore through swamps they were strafed by Batista's fighter planes. Only a dozen survived. Miraculously, they regrouped and set up their base camp and headquarters in La Plata, in the heart of the nearby Sierra Maestra mountains. Over the following two years they waged a protracted war against Batista's troops which culminated on 31st December, 1958, when a military train loaded with artillery was captured by the rebels in Santa Clara. Hours later, Batista fled Cuba. The campaign to overthrow him had claimed the lives of approximately 20,000 people.

The new government was swift to carry out far-reaching reforms of the health and education systems, which were expanded with the aim of giving improved access to the majority of the population. The economy too was reformed. Large companies, including foreign-owned concerns and landholdings, were nationalised. The Cuban authorities offered to enter into negotiations, but U.S. officials rejected the offer. Tensions surfaced between Havana and Washington, which soon crystallised into hostility. In January 1961 Washington announced that it was cutting diplomatic relations with Cuba. While Castro and his rebel-leaders-turned- government-ministers were consolidating their revolutionary changes, plans were afoot in the U.S. to overthrow them. Tens of thousands of disgruntled Cubans had gone into exile and many of them were willing recruits in numerous sabotage attempts. The most famous was the Bay of Pigs invasion in April 1961 when 1,500 CIA-trained counter revolutionaries launched an invasion that landed in Playa Girón on the Caribbean coast of Cuba. They were defeated in three days.

The Bay of Pigs was a major turning point. Castro's victory increased his standing among his own people and also with the broad spectrum of left-wing and progressive groups internationally. On the upsurge of popular support, he proclaimed the Cuban revolution Socialist in nature on the eve of the Bay of Pigs attack, which inflamed relations with the U.S. even further. Over the next fifty years the United States proved relentless in pursuing its determination to undermine the Cuban revolution. Sabotage, espionage, biological and propaganda warfare has failed to bring down Castro's government, as have the direct attempts on the Cuban leader's life. However, this campaign, together with the decades-long economic blockade, has taken a very heavy toll on the lives and the health of the Cuban population. The cost of defending the revolution is estimated at between $40 and $50 million USD, a very high price for an island population of 11.2 million people.

This is the hostile backdrop against which the Cuban regime has endeavoured to consolidate and expand the revolution. In the early 1960s cooperatives were formed throughout the island, a national literacy campaign was launched in which around a hundred thousand volunteers travelled into the countryside to teach young and old to read and write. Doctors and teachers had to be trained to replace those who had gone into exile with tens of thousands of other upper and middle-class professionals. Mass organisations were formed to mobilise the population as part of a network of civil defence, the largest being the Committees for the Defence of the Revolution (CDRs). Every block in every neighbourhood throughout the island belongs to this network. A nationwide Federation of Cuban Women (FMC) was established and children and youth organisations were set up. The only recognised political party is the Communist Party.

For thirty years developments in both the economic and the political spheres on the island were determined in varying degrees by relations between Havana and Moscow. Shiploads of sugar were traded for Russian oil in an agreement that was favourable to the Cubans. During that period tens of thousands of Cuban students completed their university degrees and post graduates in Eastern bloc countries. A number of Russian professionals doing overseas service on the island eventually settled there, marrying

Cuban nationals and making Cuba their home. In 1990 this era ended when President Mikhail Gorbachov declared that trade between Cuba and the Soviet Union would henceforth be ruled by market prices, as opposed to the previous friendly nation terms. Within weeks the Cuban economy went into freefall. Over eighty per cent of Cuba's trade with its powerful partner vanished and standards of living on the island plummeted. Fidel Castro named the emergency a "Special Period in Times of Peace."

Draconian measures were passed aimed at ensuring not just the survival of the revolution, but of its people. There were widespread cutbacks in fuel supplies, spare parts vanished and electricity blackouts, lasting up to eighteen hours, became common. People routinely waited hours for buses and over a million bikes were imported from China to alleviate the transport crisis. Food was strictly rationed. The average Cuban lost 8 – 10 kilos in weight and some children suffered symptoms of malnutrition. Animals, especially cats, disappeared from the streets in a country desperate for protein. In 1993, the worst year of the Special Period, Fidel Castro made two historic announcements aimed at capturing much-needed hard currency: ownership of the dollar would be legalised and priority would be given to the development of tourism as the key sector in the economy, as opposed to sugar cane. The following year, over thirty thousand desperate Cubans took to the sea in boats and an array of homemade vessels, endeavouring to reach the United States - and hopefully a better life. An agreement was drawn up the following year between both countries aimed at regulating the exodus.

While the Cuban government was addressing the traumatic changes facing the country, the U.S. took advantage of the crisis to intensify its efforts to destabilise the revolution. In 1992, the Torricelli Law was passed, strengthening the blockade even further, and four years later the Helms-Burton Law decreed that any American travelling to Cuba could be fined $50,000 USD. In 1997 a plague of

Thrips Palmi, an insect which is highly dangerous to a range of crops, was identified in the Matanzas region, just east of Havana. The insect is indigenous to Asia and had never previously appeared on the island. Cuban authorities linked the infestation with a U.S. registered crop duster aircraft seen operating suspiciously in the area two months previously. An official protest was made to the U.S. Interests Section in Havana at the time.

The Cuban revolution has always defined itself as international in character, hence its involvement in Africa, chiefly Angola, Ethiopia and Mozambique, in Central America, and Latin America in the 1970s and 1980s. These days it is mainly doctors, as opposed to troops and military advisors, who complete overseas missions. A large number are currently posted to Venezuela in a health-for-oil agreement with Hugo Chávez's government. Back in Havana the Latin American School of Medicine (ELAM), accepts students, mainly but not exclusively, from developing countries to train as doctors. The school, which was opened in 1999, is free and grant-aided. Between 10,000 and 12,000 young people study and board there. There is also the International School of Cinema and Television (EICTV), which offers extended training programmes to professionals and students from all over the world.

No official end has been declared to the "Special Period in Time of Peace" and its legacy continues. While the country has survived the worst effects of the economic crisis, widespread shortages are still apparent. Medicine is perhaps the most critical. Pharmacies are depressing places to visit, including those that trade in hard currency. Acquiring equipment of practically any type requires a long wait. Food prices in hard currency supermarkets are high and there is a general lack of choice. Spare parts are often very difficult to come by and Cuban mechanics have become magicians in the art of keeping decades-old vehicles on the road. Queues everywhere attest to the lack of supply and the constant demand.

From the moment the traveller arrives in Cuba, it is abundantly apparent that there is hardship. To what extent the widespread poverty is a consequence of the long-standing U.S. blockade is not clear. That the economy has been crippled because of it is undeniable. This was the purpose in implementing it fifty years ago. What is also not clear is the extent to which the threat from the United States has impacted upon human rights in Cuba. Leaving speculation aside, it is reasonable to surmise that given the magnitude of the threat, the atmosphere of vulnerability and fear on the island is not ideal for promoting tolerance and flexibility. A threat "from within" cannot be taken lightly while the menace "from without" is so powerful and so prevalent. These are the complex and powerful dynamics ruling a society accused of human rights abuses and a dictatorship. And these are the forces ruling the everyday lives of people caught up in this dramatic historical conjuncture which is contemporary Cuba.

KEY DATES IN THE REVOLUTION

1st January, 1959 – Fulgencio Batista flees Havana, thereby ending a dictatorship that started with a coup d'état over six years previously. A new government of rebel leaders takes power.

17th May, 1959 – The Law of Agrarian Reform is signed. Large landowners lose out.

6th August, 1960 – A programme of nationalisation of foreign companies is implemented.

7th May, 1960 - Cuba and the Soviet Union re-establish diplomatic relations.

28th September, 1960 – Committees for the Defence of the Revolution (CDR) are set up.

20th October, 1960 – U.S.A. announces an embargo on Cuban exports.

1st January, 1961 - The National Literacy Campaign is launched in which tens of thousands of volunteer tutors participate.

3rd January, 1961 – U.S.A. severs diplomatic relations with Cuba.

16th April, 1961 – Fidel Castro announces that the Cuban revolution is socialist in nature.

17th – 19th April, 1961 -The Bay of Pigs invasion is defeated in Cuba.

3rd February, 1962 - U.S. President John F. Kennedy orders a complete blockade of Cuba.

22nd October, 1962 – President Kennedy orders a total blockade of all vessels to the island carrying weapons in response to the deployment of medium-range Soviet missiles in Cuba. One week later Russian president Nikita Khrushchev orders his Cuba-bound fleet to return to port, thereby avoiding a confrontation between the two superpowers.

1969 – 1970 – A countrywide endeavour to achieve a sugar harvest of ten million tons fails.

5th November, 1975 - Cuba sends its first troops to Angola.

17th – 22nd December, 1975 – A new Constitution is approved and Fidel Castro is elected Secretary General of the Communist Party of Cuba (PCC) at the 1st Congress.

3rd December, 1976 – Fidel Castro is elected president of Cuba.

April 1980 - Approximately 10,000 Cubans occupy the Peruvian embassy causing a crisis that leads to the Mariel boatlift in which 130,000 Cubans embark on voyages taking them north, to the United States.

15th December, 1984 – Cuba and the United States sign an agreement in New York on migration.

May 1985 – Radio Martí, based in the United States, begins to broadcast counter-revolutionary propaganda specifically aimed at Cuba. In response, Castro's government suspends the migration agreements.

22nd December, 1988 – Peace agreements signed in Africa signal the start of Cuban troop withdrawal from Angola. The last soldiers return home in May 1991.

25th June, 1990 – President Mikhail Gorbachov announces that as from January 1991 trade relations between his country and Cuba would be governed by market prices.

29th August, 1990 – Fidel Castro declares that the economic crisis is a "Special Period in Times of Peace" and announces a series of austerity measures.

24th June, 1992 – U.S. Congress approves the Torricelli Law, drawn up to tighten the blockade of Cuba by prohibiting the foreign subsidiaries of U.S. companies from trading with Cuba.

9th August, 1993 – In the worst year of the Special Period, ownership of the U.S. dollars is legalised in Cuba.

August, 1994 – Fidel Castro orders the coast guard not to prevent the exit of people in boats, many of which are homemade. Tens of thousands take to the seas. The U.S. transports 32,000 to its base in Guantanamo while others end up in Panama.

2nd May, 1995 – A migration agreement between Cuba and the United States ends the "crisis of the boat people."

12th March, 1996 – U.S. President Bill Clinton signs the Helms-Burton Law which threatens to sue foreign companies doing business with Cuba and to fine U.S. citizens travelling to Cuba.

21st – 25th December, 1998 – Pope John Paul II visits Cuba.

30th October, 2000 – President Hugo Chávez of Venezuela and Fidel Castro sign an agreement in Caracas in which Venezuelan oil is exchanged for the services of Cuban personnel, chiefly doctors.

10th May, 2002 – Leading Cuban dissident Osvaldo Payá presents his petition for change, the Varela Project, to the national assembly.

13th May, 2002 – Former U.S. President Jimmy Carter arrives in Cuba on a good will visit. He makes a speech calling on the U.S. to end its blockade of the island and mentions the Varela Project for change in Cuba.

27th June, 2002 – Following a nationwide referendum the Cuban parliament amends the Constitution, making socialism permanent.

18th March, 2003 – A total of 75 dissidents are detained and condemned to prison.

11th April, 2001 – Three hijackers are executed in Havana. A further four are given life sentences for hijacking a small passenger boat with fifty people aboard in an attempt to reach the U.S. coast. Prior to this a number of aircraft had been hijacked and flown to the United States..

8th November, 2004 - The U.S. dollar is withdrawn and the only hard currency in circulation is the Cuban convertible peso (CUC), also known as a *chavito*.

31st July, 2006 - Due to illness Fidel Castro hands the presidency over to his younger brother Raúl, on a temporary basis.

19th February, 2008 - Fidel Castro declares that he will not be resuming his leadership positions within government.

24th February, 2008 - Raúl Castro is elected president of Cuba.

Explanatory Notes On Some Of The Organisations Mentioned In This Book

Granma International is the weekly newspaper of the Central Committee of the Communist Party of Cuba and sister newspaper of *Granma* daily. It is much closer to a bulletin than a newspaper in the sense that information contained in it is brief, generally summarising news and events, unless the full version of one of government leader's speeches is published. Until 1991 the newspaper was called *Weekly Review* and thereafter *Granma International*. Its title is in reference to the yacht *Granma*, which Fidel and 81 other rebels used in 1956 to make the crossing from Mexico to the Oriente province in the east of Cuba, the starting point of their revolution. In addition to the speeches, the newspaper typically contains information on the economy and industry, features on Cuban history, a synopsis of international news, official announcements, sports and television programmes. The newspaper is also published in digital version in Spanish, English, French, German, Portuguese, and latterly in Italian. Native language speakers are recruited to work as translators and paid a monthly stipend of around $120 USD*, in addition to free accommodation and all the rights of ordinary Cuban citizens, such as subsidised food and free health care. The minimum period of contract is one year but a number stay on in Cuba for much longer, and some never leave

* While I was working there in 1999-2000.

Committees for the Defence of the Revolution (CDRs) - On 28th September, 1960, Fidel Castro announced the formation of a nationwide network of hierarchically integrated neighbourhood committees. There would be one on every block and citizens become a member once they are fourteen years old, meaning that over seven million Cubans belong to the CDRs at some level. As their title indicates, the CDRs exist for the defence the revolution. Defence entails, above all, vigilance. Newcomers must register with the CDR, even if they are only visiting briefly. Suspicious activities, unusual gatherings, movement of people or objects have to be reported to the CDR president. A night-time guard is mounted in the area every evening in which residents are expected to participate. Women are not assigned all-night shifts. The CDR is also responsible for organising voluntary clean ups of the neighbourhood, as well as recycling campaigns, health promotion events and blood donation drives. Cubans emigrating from the island in the early 1990s, during the worst years of the economic crisis, were frequently jeered by mobs in "acts of repudiation" organised by the CDRs. Critics of the CDRs say they are networks that encourage people to spy on each other and inform the authorities.

The **Federation of Cuban Women (FMC)** is a non-governmental organisation operating at local, provincial and national level throughout the island for the defence of women's rights. Membership includes around 80 per cent of women over the age of fourteen, although only a minority is actively involved in the activities of the organisation. Women's health, education and equality form the basis of FMC campaigns.

Cuban Institute for Friendship among Peoples (ICAP) was established in 1961 to strengthen and promote links between Cuba and international solidarity organisations. One of the ways in which it does this is through volunteer work brigades whose members typically spend up to a month in Cuba. ICAP also has its own travel agency, Amistur, which designs programmes and organises tours for solidarity groups interested in visiting the island.

Communist Party of Cuba (PCC) is the only recognised

political party in Cuba. It was formed in 1965 from the merger of a number of small revolutionary organisations. The first Party Congress was held in 1975, by which time the membership had grown to 200,000 members and since then ranks have swollen to around 800,000 members.[vi] The Central Committee – the ruling council – comprises around 150 leading members of the Party. The Castro brothers, Fidel and Raúl, held the positions of first and second secretary respectively from 1965 until 2008, when Fidel resigned due to ill health. His brother substituted him at that point in the leadership position. Following the collapse of the Soviet Union there was a shift in focus in PCC ideology a few degrees away from Marx and Lenin, towards the Cuban 19th century hero and intellectual José Martí and home-grown radicalism,. Applications for membership of the PCC are vetted and scrutinised.

U.S. Interests Section – is a de facto embassy operating in the absence of formal diplomatic relations between the two countries. It is located on the premises of the Swiss embassy, an ugly bunker-style building on the Havana seafront. Staffed by both Cuban and American workers, security in and around the building is extremely tight. Blue-uniformed Cuban police suspiciously eye passers by and approaching vehicles. A large bill board erected opposite the bombproof windows blasts out the words *We have absolutely no fear of you Mr Imperialists.**

*This is reported to have been removed in 2009.

The International Press Centre (CPI) is based on the Rampa in Havana and is run by the Ministry of Foreign Affairs (MINREX). Journalists, photographers and camera crew planning to work in Cuba request accreditation via the Cuban embassy in their country of origin. If the application is approved they are issued with a visa for media workers and a press card, and they are expected to register with the CPI on arrival in Havana. According to the CPI website around 159 foreign residents from 32 countries belong to the permanent press corps while over 1,500 temporary press visas are issued annually to visiting journalists.

Global Exchange is a San Francisco-based organisation that campaigns for international human rights and global justice. A key part of its work involves organising educational tours, reality tours, which give participants an opportunity to gain first hand experience of cultures and societies that are engaged in political, economic, environmental and economic challenges. The focus of the tours is both educational and solidarity. American citizens wishing to travel to Cuba are subject to severe restrictions by their own government. They may only travel under a special licence agreement, which Global Exchange has been granted for its tours.

http://www.globalexchange.org/tours/by-country?field_country_nid=134

Notes

[i]   General Augusto Pinochet (1915-2006) staged a right-wing coup d'état in Chile on 11 September, 1973. He overthrew Salvador Allende, the democratically-elected president, who was killed in the battle, and began a bloody dictatorship that lasted until 1990. The regime used torture and disappearances to suppress the population. Tens of thousands went into exile.

ii   Pablo Neruda (1904-1973), who won the Nobel prize for Literature in 1971, is considered to be one of the most influential writers of his generation. He was a member of the Chilean Communist Party.

iii   Víctor Jara (1932-1973) was a renowned Chilean protest singer who was tortured and murdered by the military regime in the days following the coup in Chile. He was a member of the Chilean Communist Party.

iv   Around 37,000 Cuban troops were deployed to Angola during the period 1986-1991 in support of the People's Movement for the Liberation of Angola (MPLA) against the National Union for the Total Independence of Angola (UNITA). Cuba was the MPLA's main ally, while South Africa backed the forces of UNITA.

v   http://www.elcato.org/cuba-educacion-en-crisis

        http://news.bbc.co.uk/hi/spanish/specials/2006/educacion/newsid_4818000/4818322.stm

        http://www.juventudrebelde.cu/cuba/2006-11-05/mas-de-90-000-maestros-emergentes-incorporados-a-las-aulas/

vi   http://congresopcc.cip.cu/

CPSIA information can be obtained
at www.ICGtesting.com
Printed in the USA
LVOW01s1943140916
504616LV00025B/480/P